MAHAKAL
EXPERIENCE & ECSTASY

Pinky Raj Sah

Qurate
quratebooks.com

MAHAKAL EXPERIENCE & ECSTASY

Pinky Raj Sah

Published in 2024

© Published by

qurate
quratebooks.com

Qurate Books Pvt. Ltd.
Goa 403523, India
www.quratebooks.com
Tel: 1800-210-6527, Email: info@quratebooks.com

ISBN: 978-93-58983-17-3

DEDICATED TO
LORD MAHAKAL

Foreword

Infinite reverence to Lord Mahakal, the Supreme God of Gods, Trilokinath, Shiv-Shambhu, Trikaldarshi, Ashutosh, Kaljayi, Kaal of Kaal, Bhootbhavan , Bholenath.

Every glory of Lord Mahakal is immeasurable, as through a mere darshan (glimpse) one gets the result of pious virtues of many births.

An exemplary meaningful effort of such an international religious spiritual deity has been made to bring out every aspect of Lord Mahakal through this book by the writer Ms. Pinky Raj Sah. This book is a magnificent endeavor in bringing out the essence of Lord Mahakal's magnificence; Mahakal whose majesty is boundless and whose divine glory is matched only by the infinite universe.

This book written with passion and dedication is a remarkable tribute to the greatness and glory of Baba Mahakal.

The author, a devotee of Baba Mahakal, has included in this book her attraction towards Mahakal, history, miracles, mythological stories associated with Baab Mahakal, temple architecture, the priest dynasty, religious traditions, Bhasma aarti, Mahakal's ageless philosophies and other important aspects related to Mahakal. Statements of Baba Mahakal's devotees have been added beautifully illuminating the grandeur of Baba

Mahakal and add a personal touch to the sacred tone of the book making it a treasured companion.

Through her meticulous writing, the author has woven a narrative that is both informative and captivating. She has made a meaningful and commendable effort to include all aspects of Baba Mahakal with all HIS grandeur and mystique.

Being born and brought up in the world's most ancient, mythological, religious, spiritual, and cultural city of Ujjain, writing this foreword, I am filled with gratitude for the opportunity to be a part of this awesome endeavor.

I extend my heartfelt blessings to Ms. Pinky Raj Sah, who has poured her heart and soul into this book. Through her book she has offered the flowers of her faith towards Lord Mahakal, who is present in every particle of the devotees around the globe. May it be a source of inspiration and devotion to all who read it.

It is my wish to Lord Mahakal to bless this book with his divine presence, and may it remain a cherished companion to all who seek to deepen their understanding of this sacred deity and may the fame of the author forever be synonymous with literary excellence and devotion to the Supreme Lord Mahakal and flow on the world stage.

Dr. Anil Prem Junwal

Subedar (M)

IGP Office Ujjain Zone (M.P. Police)

Chief Editor and author of "Hindi key Naye Charan"&" Rajbhasha Chetna"

Editor: International Research Paper - Vindhyan Bloom, Rhythm & Vivekanand

Author of Poetry folder "Maa"," Betiya"& "Ram Vandana"

Author of over 20+ research papers

Thank You Guruji

Pujari Mahesh Ji

(Khootpaati Juna Brahmin Head)

Pujari Mahesh Ji was born on June 24, 1956, in Ujjain, into a revered family of Khootpaati pujaris, his father late Sh. Prem Narayan Pujari, and his mother, late Smt. Rukmani Devi. His journey into spirituality began early, as he started visiting the Mahakaleshwar temple from the tender age of two holding his father's hands. For almost 64 years now, he has dedicated himself to serving Lord Mahakal with unwavering devotion.

Initially pursuing studies in science at graduation level, Mahesh Ji's path took a turn after his first year of college due to his father's deteriorating health when he chose to delve deeper into Yajurveda Siksha. This decision marked the beginning of his lifelong commitment to spiritual learning and service to not only Lord Mahakal but towards mankind.

Mahesh Ji is not only a revered figure in Ujjain but also holds a significant stature among religious communities nationwide. He is known for his leadership as the head of Mahakal Sena, an initiative aimed at uniting all India pujaris under the umbrella of Sanatan Dharma to preserve and promote its timeless culture along with establishing Akhil Bhartiya Yuva Brahmin Samaj. He has built Parshuram temple, Jhansi ki Rani statue and Chanakya puri colony. Guruji has also received many "upadhis" and recognitions from various organizations for his innumerous contributions to society at large.

Throughout my journey, every encounter reaffirmed that Mahesh Guruji is an unparalleled source of insight into every facet of Lord Mahakal. Meeting him feels like a blessing from Mahakal himself, guiding me to articulate the truth about Baba Mahakal without the distortion of myths or half-truths.

Thank you, Guruji, for imparting your wisdom and allowing me to share your profound knowledge with others.

Acknowledgement

I dedicate this book to LORD MAHAKAL

My deepest reverence to Lord Mahakal himself, whose timeless wisdom and boundless grace has guided me on this profound journey of exploration and self-discovery.

Writing this book on Lord Mahakal has been a deeply fulfilling journey, and I am grateful to everyone who has contributed to its realization.

I extend my sincere thanks to Mahesh Guru ji, whose unwavering support, knowledge & encouragement sustained me throughout the writing process. Your expertise and guidance has enriched the content of this book immeasurably & your belief in me inspired me to delve deeper into the mysteries of Mahakal.

My heartfelt thanks to Ms. Manita Rai, DSP Ujjain Police, for sparing her valuable time in sharing her experiences with me and also for being a source of inspiration and motivation.

I would also like to extend my gratitude to Dr. Anil Prem Junwal (Ujjain Police) for his unwavering support, feedback and enthusiasm for my book.

I am indebted to Pujari Vijay Ji, whose insights were invaluable in bringing clarity to complex concepts. With your jovial nature you have encouraged me in every way you could.

My thanks to other esteemed pujaris of Mahakaleshwar temple who graciously shared their invaluable knowledge and time.

I am grateful for the expertise and guidance extended by the entire publishing team at Qurate. Your careful attention to detail, relentless effort, professional guidance and zeal for the book have been invaluable.

I would also like to express my gratitude to people from all walks of life who wholeheartedly shared their experiences of Baba Mahakal with me, which has contributed significantly to the completion of this book and have added to the depth of my faith in Lord Mahakal.

Last but not the least to my family and friends, thank you for your patience, understanding, and encouragement during the countless hours away from home spent researching and writing. Your unwavering support means the world to me.

This book is a testament to the collective effort and support of all those mentioned and many others who have touched my life along the way. Thank you all for being a valuable part of this journey.

Pinky Raj Sah

Contents

(With real life experiences of Mahakal devotees)

Introduction

In the heart of the bustling markets and narrow lanes of Ujjain, where devotees chant solemn hymns, I discovered the true meaning of life. With each morning rays of the sun, casting hues of gold over the majestic Mahakaleshwar, I realized that my journey had only just begun.

For some unknown reason, the first time I arrived at Ujjain, the anticipation and excitement of Mahakal's darshan (glimpse) settled upon me like a comforting blanket with his first gaze.

And I knew exactly where I was and what I had discovered.

Mahakal's influence is omnipresent. In his world, hours, days, and years become meaningless. The past, present, and future all mix together like a big jigsaw puzzle. This is the domain of Mahakal, where time is king and nothing stays the same for long.

This mystical figure Mahakal - the lord of time and death, fascinates and inspires people from all cultures and time. He embodies the ancient Shiva of mythology, but he is also the Shiva of the present - the universal presence that dwells in our hearts, eternally modern. Mahakal's glory and HIS captivating charm draws countless devotees to him with tears of joy leading their life to a positive direction. Fascination with Mahakal is something personal and untouched. It stems not only from HIS role as a central figure in Hindu mythology but also from the profound relevance of his teachings in today's world, the universal truths that resonate across cultures and generations.

This tribute to Mahakal is intertwined with the personal experiences and insights of Mahakal's devotees, historical accounts, and the rituals of Mahakaleshwar along with my own experience. Let's embark on a journey to unravel Mahakal's mysticism and profound wisdom along with His timeless essence viewing it as a journey towards self-improvement and discovery.

Join me on this beautiful but ongoing journey into the heart of Mahakal's kingdom, where the threads of fate change, for in HIS realm, nothing is as it seems.

May Mahakal inspire you to think about life's mysteries, understand yourself better, and uncover the limitless depths of divine spirituality.

CHAPTER 1

My Attraction to Mahakal

Being born into a typical Hindu family, God has always been present in my life. I grew up praying to God first thing in the morning before going to school - that was my upbringing. Like all other girls my favourite deity was Shiva. Over time, I became engrossed in Durga and Krishna. Although all Gods are one, we mere mortals give them different names and appearances based on our own convictions.

Though never completely forgotten, Shiva faded into the background over time.

Mahakal……. I had never heard of in my half century of life, except occasionally at the mention of the 12 Jyotirlings by others... Yes, until a few months ago Mahakal was not even in my slightest imagination.

They say everything is predestined, and now I really believe it. One event leads to another. Not too long ago, my father and our family priest were insisting us to take our elder daughter to Mahakal and encouraged me to start offering Jal (water) to Shiva at any nearby temple. Suddenly, my long-forgotten devotion to Shiva took precedence again.

It was probably the first time I heard of Mahakal, though I could not understand what Mahakal actually means or who HE is, except that he is Shiva. Initially, my husband was supposed to take our daughter to Mahakal, but could not due to his professional commitments (well that's what we thought at that time) so I agreed to go considering it as just another normal temple visit. But destiny had other plans – plans beyond human comprehension.

Only later did I understand that it was Mahakal's will & that HE wanted me to come. (It is believed that only those can have His darshan who are called by Him otherwise no matter how hard you try you will come back without his darshan even from his temple).

Thinking of it as a holiday, but without a train reservation and after days of unsuccessful attempts to get tickets, I sat in our home temple and tearfully asked Shiva why I could not go, even though Mahakal had no meaning for me at that point. Miraculously, same afternoon yes you read it right same afternoon I discovered an alternative, albeit longer, train route through a relative and without losing a moment I booked the tickets.

Before I knew, my younger daughter and I (not the elder one who was actually supposed to go) were on our way to Ujjain. My husband had urged me to book tickets for the Bhasma Aarti, which was a challenge as it requires prior booking. I talked to few people in Ujjain for Bhasma Aarti but none could confirm. Nevertheless, by Mahakal's will somehow our 4 am Bhasma Aarti protocol tickets were arranged (about which I came to know only after reaching Ujjain). Getting down at Ujjain at 9 pm with only a three hour rest, at midnight my daughter & I were sitting in the Bhasma Aarti queue as per the standard protocol. Unexpectedly, while waiting in the queue without cell phones, (cell phones have to be put in a locker) I struck up conversations with people from different regions of India who had their own reasons for being there.

At that point of time I had no way of knowing that this chance occurrence would have a lasting significance on my life.

And now begins the real anecdote ....

As the sun prepared to rise over the ancient city of Ujjain, casting its golden glow over the revered site, I found myself transported to a realm beyond the mundane being enveloped in an atmosphere of profound inner peace and fulfilment.

It was as if the universe had conspired to bring me to this sacred spot, where the essence of Mahakal, the mighty god of time and death, is palpable. Amidst thousands of devotees, I stood at the middle of the threshold of the upper floor, right in the front row from where Mahakal was visible clearly and at His best, HIS presence manifesting before my very eyes.

Was this mere coincidence?

Could it be called divine intervention?

The wait was long, the crowd dense, yet anticipation hung in the air.

As the Bhasma Aarti unfolded, the sacred ritual enveloped all in a kaleidoscope of devotional fervor. The reverberating chants, pulsating drumbeats and manjeera sounds harmonized in a majestic symphony, bathing the deity in an aura of divine splendor. Amidst this grandeur, I found myself lost in the reverberations of the ritual, my soul responding with an unbridled intensity.

With the sacred hymns washing over me, tears began to flow from my eyes, untethered by the confines of rational thought. In that moment, it was as if Mahakal and I were the sole occupants of a universe without bounds - no distractions, no interruptions, no echoes of the mundane, I felt one with the deity, suspended in an eternal devotion.

It was like an unprecedented magnetic pull, a force drawing me in, to which I willingly surrendered. It was a manifestation of Shiva's form I had never before encountered, a manifestation that had been waiting to reveal itself to me.

Even after the Aarti concluded, I remained rooted to the spot, reluctant to break free from the grip of this mystical encounter.

The experience had left an indelible mark on my being, infusing me with a sense of depth and understanding that transcended the realm of the ordinary. I felt like my soul remained suspended in the hallowed space where Mahakal and I had communed.

Time lost all meaning as I dwelled in the presence of the eternal. The encounter had unearthed a hidden dimension within me, one that would forever be linked to the majesty of Mahakal and the mystery of HIS form.

It's as if the cosmos had orchestrated this encounter, guiding me to this threshold of understanding. The phrase "divine intervention" took on a new meaning here. It's not just a casual remark; it's a testament to the mystical forces that had brought me to this juncture.

In the radiance of Mahakal's presence, I was reminded of the realities of life and the eternal cycle of birth, growth, decay, and rebirth.

I was granted a glimpse into the timeless tapestry of existence in this mystical confluence. Something in my soul was stirred by the realization that every moment is a chance to transcend, to renew, and to awaken to the mystery that lies at the heart of all existence.

This is not just an experience; it's a realization. And as I stood before Mahakal, I knew that my life had been forever changed by this encounter. The essence of time and mortality has been distilled within me, and I seemed to have emerged transformed, with a newfound appreciation for the preciousness of each moment.

This was no ordinary encounter; it was a spiritual awakening that would stay with me till eternity.

Even as the last notes of the aarti slowly receded there was a moment of stillness in which I found myself difficult to move so deeply immersed was I in the sacred experience.

As I slowly returned to the world of the living, I took in the diverse reactions of those around me. Some were deeply absorbed in the spiritual atmosphere, their eyes closed in rapt attention, their faces aglow with an otherworldly light, others however, seemed oblivious to the profound energy that had just enveloped us, their gaze fixed instead on the screens of their mobile devices, as if trying to capture the moment for showing off on social media, few others around me were frustrated and agitated, grumbling about the crowd and the weather, seemingly more concerned with their immediate discomfort than the transcendental experience unfolding before them.

As I looked around, I realized that each of us had been touched by the experience in our own unique way - some more consciously aware of its significance, others perhaps only dimly sensing its presence and some totally unaware, despite these varied reactions, we were all united in this moment, connected by a shared experience that would linger within us long after we left the sacred site behind.

Sitting in the temple premises I was thinking as to why I was here? What was the reason that I had been blessed to experience an out of this world experience? I have always believed that everything in this world happens for a reason. Even though we may not be able to recognize the reason in that moment, nothing conspires without it. I sat wondering about it nevertheless too happy to have been blessed to actually feel the presence of Mahakal.

I didn't, but Mahakal knew why HE had called me there....

Leaving the temple, I reflected on whether it was a genuine encounter with another realm or just a fleeting moment.

Subsequent visits to other temples felt routine by comparison.

In the afternoon, an inexplicable urge drew me back to Mahakal. Another divine experience awaited me. How would you react if I told you that this time somehow events unfolded with Mahakal guiding me to sit near Nandi, his most devoted worshipper and attendant, just outside the main sanctum sanctorum (garbha griha) typically reserved for dignitaries /protocol visitors—this blessing lasting for almost full five minutes?

It was yet another awe-inspiring moment. I was completely absorbed in Mahakal. A deep silence enveloped me, goose bumps covering my entire body. It felt as though time itself had paused, reminiscent of scenes from movies where the wind ceases and the world stands still.

Perhaps many of you reading this have experienced something similar, or something entirely different during Mahakal's darshan.

After those five minutes passed, I struggled to articulate the feeling—it was as if a lifetime had elapsed. Overwhelmed by emotions I never knew existed, I bowed to Mahakal for granting me a fresh perspective, a new found clarity in life.

If this wasn't enough, later in the evening, I found myself allured towards Mahakal again, as if some magnet was pulling me towards Him, present at His evening aarti. I was simply filled with a great sense of gratitude.

And all I could feel was ...blessed.

This was my first profound experience of Mahakal. The next day, with a heavy heart I had to depart from Ujjain for my home.

Before my first darshan of Mahakal like most people I had been struggling with unreasonable reasons be it finance, kids, simply not feeling happy, getting irritated over any and everything, about my situations, etc., etc. However, this divine encounter stirred something profound within me. I don't claim sudden transformation or newfound self-mastery, but undeniably, something within me has changed for the better ever since.

I believe HE called me there to dispel my illusions, showing that a true connection with HIM transcends mere temple worship or rituals and making me realize what real happiness is.

A month later I again felt an inexplicable urge for Mahakal's darshan.... The second time I went for Mahakal's darshan believe me nothing had changed, everything, every feeling was same as before when I was in front of Lord Mahakal. I just wanted to keep looking at Mahakal. That day I went thrice for Mahakal's darshan but I did not ask for anything from Baba, I felt that being there was a blessing in itself, and if Mahakal's blessings are with you than what more can you ask from life. And it was only later that I was to realize another reason for Him calling me to his doorstep.

Almost a day after I sat in my home temple, meditating and chanting the Shiv mantra after my second visit to Mahakal, I felt a voice urging me to express my thoughts and emotions about my experience of Mahakal through writing. I ignored the voice thinking it was just my imagination...

As fate would have it, I had left my job since the outbreak of Covid, and writing had always been a long-standing passion of mine. Yet, I had neglected it over time. Same night I woke up startled from my sleep when I heard a voice, maybe in my dreams, asking me again to write about Mahakal as I had experienced Him. Little did I know that this was the beginning of my transformative journey.

Ms. Manita Rai

DSP Ujjain

"I have been in the police for 25 years now. If you are in Ujjain and you don't visit Mahakal then it means you are incomplete. I keep going there unke bina hamara astitva hi nahi hei. Whenever I go to Mahakaleshwar temple I feel that I will ask this or that from Mahakal Baba but as soon as I am in front of Him I become speechless. I don't know what happens but all I want at that moment is to keep seeing HIM, I always feel so relaxed like HE is everything to me.

The faith I have for my God and when I involve myself in HIM that is Bhakti for me

Shiv embodies both poison as well as divine nectar same ways we humans have both the good points as well as negative ones. We need to learn to accept the good things in people and let go of the flaws this is what I feel we need to imbibe from Shiv"

Dr. Shubhangi Gatghe

Eye specialist, Pune

"It's the second time I am visiting Mahakaleshwar temple. First time I came I could not get a good darshan(view) of Baba Mahakal so I felt something was missing, hence I have come again & this time by Baba's grace I had a peaceful darshan. I feel there is a supreme power which is making everything happen, be it my coming here again or any big event worldwide. In Baba Mahakal's presence I get a feeling of security when I am in front of him, just like a daughter feels secure under her father's watchful eyes. The glow on my face is from that feeling of security.

We should all learn from Shiva to be patient, have control over our anger and toxicity."

CHAPTER 2

Experiencing Mahakal

The power I felt when I was face to face with Mahakal (during HIS darshans) is something that cannot be expressed in mere words. It's something that I felt very strongly & keep feeling whenever I have HIS darshan. During my journey of trying to get to know Mahakal, (it's never enough...the more you try the less you feel you know Him) I came across people from all walks of life & from every nook & corner of India be it from Karnataka, Bengal, Gujarat or Jharkhand.... None of them had words to express how they felt, but all had felt an energy - a positive energy that drew them to Mahakal and all unanimously agreed that something good always happens to them after Mahakal's darshan. Of course there were many who had come there only as a holiday to the sacred place but they were the ones who in spite of being blessed by Mahakal for HIS darshan could not make use of the blessing ...maybe they didn't see the chance for something unknowingly better being given to them by Mahakal himself because not all are blessed to go to Mahakal no matter how hard they try while some who go for Mahakal darshan regularly say that they are drawn by Mahakal Himself and feel really blessed. I am one of them. I feel really blessed to have the chance to be in Mahakal's presence time and again for without HIS call I cannot approach HIS threshold and every time I go there I feel a positive energy inside me. I have learnt or rather discovered a few facts about life itself which I had generally ignored in spite of those realities always being present.

A life changing and eye opening visit. In front of Mahakal I felt like I was a zero....in that moment one realizes that he/she is nothing in this vast universe and Mahakal is all there is, life unfolds in the most educative way...all your ego with all its attachments and pretensions vanishes into thin air when you realize that life is nothing but a fleeting moment and that all the material things you are in the race to amass will be left behind one day. One may not see the bigger changes but small positive changes are bound to come in your life after your visit to Mahakal, slowly unfolding into bigger positive happenings and changes. These changes may seem subtle at first, but they can gradually build upon one another, leading to more significant transformations in one's life. It's as if Mahakal's presence awakens a new sense of inner strength, resilience, and purpose.

One might simply understand and let go of his/her ego, or stop being too angry over small, small things, or may start living in the present fostering a greater appreciation for the present moment. Rather than worrying about the future or dwelling on the past, one becomes more grounded in the here and now after being in Mahakal's presence experiencing peace, contentment, and an inner joy. I felt like I was nothing. Actually if we think about it keeping our egos aside, we are literally nothing in this huge expanse of the universe. Being in front of Mahakal was the moment all ego inside me suddenly ceased to exist and I was only left with awe & reverence ... I felt like I was enlightened in my own small way.... Not necessary that one has to have a HALO around them to let the world know that they are enlightened as I experienced true spiritual growth and awareness in my quiet, personal moments, without requiring any external validation or recognition. I didn't have the need to seek external confirmation but embraced the internal shift that occurred within me with no doubts raised.

It's as if some magic is happening you just have to believe in that magic....something extraordinary, something unexpected takes place for the better. You just have to feel it and accept it with trust and an open mind and heart.

Looking back, I believe this was the universe's way of prompting me towards self-discovery, real happiness, getting to know Mahakal and sharing HIS timeless wisdom with others. His philosophies, which have stood the test of time across generations, are more relevant today than ever. It is as if the world has forgotten the essence of these teachings, making them an urgent need for this generation.

Now I feel that the presence of Mahakal is so strong that it shakes you to the core, burns everything to ashes and drives you towards ultimate liberation provided you are ready to believe in HIM.

Such is the power of MAHAKAL

Vijay Pujariji

Mahakaleshwar temple, Ujjain

"Bhakti is faith and the center of our trust. In bhakti one should not deviate one should do bhakti with concentration and your faith is your concentration. Bhakti will remove all obstacles from your life and solve all your problems. If today's generation is finding bhakti outdated, then somewhere the fault lies with the older generation who have not inculcated those values from childhood in their kids but have attached them towards modernism. In this fast paced world they will meet obstacles and face problems in life which can only be solved through bhakti as God shows the way to come out of any problematic situation but that needs faith and some amount of bhakti.

Shiva is the center point from where everything starts and ends, if you take away one "small maatra" from Shiv it becomes Shav. Believe in Shiva and you will find real happiness."

Ramesh Bhai

78 years, Gujarat

"I feel I had a divine experience at Mahakal. Something positive triggered in me. At this age I feel even if we do everything, it's all temporary, only Bhakti is permanent. I hope young people realize this the sooner the better instead of going after the rat race. Shiv is the only truth. Being a part of the Bhasma aarti made all the hardships & efforts I had to go through in coming here at my age worth it. I feel complete now. No regrets even if I die now for I have had the blessing of Mahakal's darshan"

CHAPTER 3

Unveiling Mahakal

Who is Mahakal? Is he synonymous with Shiv, or are they distinct entities or various manifestations of the same divine essence?

Scholars and religious figures have extensively agreed that Shiva and Mahakal are essentially one, appearing in different forms.

Mahakal is Shiva and Shiva is Mahakal.

A shloka in Ling Purana also highlights Mahakal as synonymous with Shiva, emphasizing his eternal and supreme nature in the context of timelessness and spiritual welfare.

Kaal means a time-period. Mahakal means someone who is Supreme and above the time-period or the boundaries of time. Representing Lord Shiva, Mahakal embodies the concept of time itself, often described as surpassing both time and death. There's nothing beyond him, no element, no confines, not indeed time (kaal).

Mahakal is the epitome of Lord Shiva and embodies the role of the ultimate destroyer of all elements. The prefix "maha" means great, while "kaal" denotes time and symbolizes Shiva as the supreme guardian of time. Kaal also means death, so Mahakal can be interpreted as a harbinger of the ultimate (final) moment of death, the dissolution of all existence.

In Mahakal limitations imposed by time dissolve, unveiling boundless possibilities. The journey from finite to infinite unfolds under HIS guidance. Even poison quivers in his presence, and resurrection emerges from the depths of oblivion, awakening fundamental truths within our consciousness and soul. Mahakal, the personification of Lord Shiva, is the destroyer of all rudiments, beyond which there's no actuality, no confines, and no conception of kaal (time). He's the ultimate reality.

Mahakal represents Shiva as the benevolent when associated with his family. In the realm of time & death Shiva assumes the form of Mahakal.

Vinayak Khattri

Indore

"Your body has a positive energy when you come here which reaches its zenith once you are face to face with Lord Mahakal. I was tired when I entered the temple premises, but once I was standing in front of Baba Mahakal it felt like I was charged; my body, my mind everything seemed fully charged. It's Baba's energy which calls me here as I come every Sunday. And when I come here something good always awaits me no matter how minuscule it may be. No matter how much crowd or what the weather HE shows the way to come for his darshan."

Akaash

25 yrs, Advocate, Delhi

"This is the 4th time I am visiting Mahakal. It's a very spiritual place and when I have the darshan of Mahakal Baba I get very positive vibes...it's something which I cannot name but the feeling is something different as if your entire life rotates in front of you and you get a new vision to live and to move ahead. For me bhakti is when I can connect with the deity I believe in, when I can see myself in him. Shiv is the epitome of knowledge and faith...from him we can imbibe tyag (sacrifice) and learn patience which is much needed today as our generation gets distracted over any and every little thing easily and lose control."

CHAPTER 4

Mahakal In Mythology

As we embark on a journey to unravel the enigmatic allure of Lord Mahakal, it is essential that we first explore the fascinating origins of this mysterious entity.

References in the Shiv Purana and Skanda Purana highlight the significance of Mahakal. Pujari Mahesh Ji, revered as a living encyclopedia of Baba Mahakal in Ujjain, shared invaluable insights with me:

"The Shivlinga in Ujjain is SWAYAMBHU, meaning it is naturally occurring or self-manifested. Mahakal's presence spans across ages—Satyug - where Mahakal existed amidst Devtas (Gods) and Danavs (Demons); Treta Yug - when Ram worshipped Lord Mahakal and Hanuman fetched holy water from Kotiteerth at Mahakaleshwar temple premises for Ram's Rajyaabhishek (coronation ceremony); Dwapar Yug - when Krishna studied at Sandipani Ashram in Ujjain and worshipped Mahakaleshwar. Now, in Kalyug and beyond, Mahakal remains eternal, existing before and after."

So Mahakal is ADI ANADI, only his swaroop (form) changes.

Mahakal's emergence with the origin of the Earth:

According to mythology, it is said that when the Earth was formed, Mahakal Jyotirlinga emerged simultaneously. Mahakal is believed to be the first Shivlinga of the Earth and that salvation can be attained merely by seeking Mahakal's darshan.

Mahakal's origin as traced to Satyug:

During a period of Pralaya (cosmic dissolution), when the Earth lay in stillness, the Devtas (celestial beings) also inhabited this realm. It is said that during this time, a dispute arose between Vishnu and Brahma regarding their supremacy as the greatest deity. Initially perceived as amusement by other Devtas, the argument escalated beyond control. In response, a colossal Jyotirlinga (symbolic representation of Lord Shiva as a pillar of light) emerged before them, its origin and purpose unknown.

To settle their debate, it was decided that whoever could locate the ends of the Jyotirlinga would be considered superior. Vishnu chose to descend into the depths of the Earth, while Brahma opted to ascend towards the skies. After an extensive search, Vishnu returned, conceding his inability to find the base of the Jyotirlinga. Meanwhile, Brahma, on his journey back, enlisted the testimony of a Ketaki flower and a cow, claiming to have reached the summit and thereby asserting his victory.

Upon learning of Brahma's deceit, Shiva appeared from the Jyotirlinga in great fury. In response to Brahma's falsehood, Shiva commanded Bhairo, to sever one of Brahma's heads. Furthermore, Shiva cursed Brahma, decreeing that he would not be worshipped anywhere. Shiva also forbade the Ketaki flower from being used in His worship due to its role in the deception. The cow, held sacred among animals, was cursed so that her mouth, from which the lie had emanated, would forever consume impurities.

Hearing the curse, Brahma, Vishnu, and the other Devtas prayed fervently for forgiveness to which ultimately Shiva relented. He decreed that Brahma would be worshipped in

Pushkar, the Ketaki flower would be revered in weddings and decorations, and the cow would remain sacred throughout, except for her mouth. On Devtas' request to Shiva, one part of the Jyotirlinga ascended to the heavens for worship by the Devtas and other celestial beings in Swarga (heaven). Another part descended to Patala loka (netherworld) for veneration by serpents, yakshas, and other beings. The remaining part settled on Earth in Avantika (present-day Ujjain) as Mahakal, to be revered by humans in Mrituyuloka (the mortal realm).

A Sanskrit mantra from the Shiva Purana

तार्कलिगं स्वर्गो, हाटकेश्वरं भुवि। महाकालेश्वरं तुभ्यं, त्रैलोक्येश्वर नामतः ll

"जो भगवानब शिव आकाश में तारक, पाताल में हाटकेश्वर एवं मृत्युलोक में महाकाल बनकर विराजते हैं, उन्हें हम नमन करते हैं"

"We bow to Lord Shiva who resides as Tarakeshwar in the sky, Hatkeshwar in the underworld and Mahakal in the world of death" and honors Mahakal as the lord of the three worlds.

Another version:

According to the ancient legends, King Chandrasena was a devout worshiper of Shiva. A young boy named Shrikhar overheard the king chanting Shiva's name and expressed his desire to join in the worship. However, the guards removed him and sent him to the outskirts of the city near Shipra River. Inspired by the unwavering devotion of King Chandrasena, Shrikhar initiated his own worship using a stone as a linga, despite initial skepticism from others. Meanwhile, Shrikhar also learned of the plans of rival kings Ripudhamana and Singhaditya to attack the city with the aid of the demon king Dushan.

Dushan possessed the power of invisibility bestowed upon him by Lord Brahma. After defeating the gods, he expelled them from their celestial abodes and ventured into the beautiful forests of Avantika i.e. Avantika Van of those times.

Despite Dushan's decree to cease the worship of Shiva, the Brahmins persisted in their devotion and meditation of Lord Shiva. Infuriated by their defiance, Dushan began persecuting anyone who visited the Brahmins for worship.

The enemies eventually arrived at Avantika (Ujjain) and began oppressing the people, imposing a ban on all Vedic rituals and activities. Seeing the grave situation Shrikhar and a priest named Vriddhi along with the citizens fervently prayed to Lord Shiva for deliverance.

Witnessing the plight of the Brahmins and the people, Lord Shiva emerged from the earth and swiftly annihilated the demon and his entire army with a single utterance of "Hum".

Grateful, the people of Avanti pleaded to Lord Shiva to remain amongst them. Moved by their devotion, from that day on, Shiva resided in His light form as Mahakala in a Lingam that was formed on its own from the powers of Shiva and his consort, Parvati. Shiva also blessed his devotees and declared that people who worshipped Him in this form would be free from the fear of death and diseases. Also, they would be under the protection of Shiva himself. This event solidified Shiva as Mahakal, the defender of righteousness and the destroyer of evil.

Vishwajeet Singh

Jharkhand

"This is the first time I have come for Mahakal's darshan. Mahakal is a different experience altogether. I could feel the strong vibrations during Mahakal's darshan. It felt as if I was transported to a totally different world. Some undefined power is certainly there. I would like to come again and again to have Baba's darshan"

Pooja Bairagi

Ujjain

"I have been working for 2 years now at Mahakaleshwar temple and every day I go for Mahakal baba's darshan in the morning before starting work. When I am with baba, I forget all my worries, my problems and feel very relaxed and at peace. I don't even feel like going home. I always feel that a saaya(shadow) is always walking with me saying I am there to take care of you. I always feared going at night but ever since I have been here I feel Baba is always there with me even when it's dark so now I feel safe. Once I remember before settling here when things were not good in my life I had asked Baba to call me near him and you will not believe, but within a few days somehow I came here and without any connection I got this job at Baba's temple. There are other things which have happened to me like a miracle ever since I started working here. I feel we can learn tyag (sacrifice) from Shiv though the amount of tyag he has done we can never even think of coming anywhere even near that."

Chapter 5

Mahakaleshwar Temple

The temple of Mahakal in Ujjain the ancient city called Avantika (Padmavati, Kumudvati, Kushashthali, Amravati and Chudamani are some other ancient names of this city) venerates the Hindu deity Shiva, who is revered as Mahakaleshwar and embodies the concepts of time and death. The name Mahakaleshwar is derived from "Mahakal", which means greater than both time and death.

Mahakal jyotirlinga is referred to as "dakshinamukhi" and is unique among the twelve jyotirlingas in that it faces south - south which is supposed to be the direction of time & death exclusive to Mahakaleshwar who controls both time & death.

The historical legacy of the Mahakaleshwar temple spans several eras. Its origin as per the Puranas states that Prajapita Brahma built it. According to ancient Sanskrit texts such as the Matsya Purana and the Avanti Khanda Mahakaleshwar temple dates back to the 4th - 6th century BC, illustrating its antiquity. During the Gupta Empire and the subsequent post-Gupta period the temple experienced an architectural heyday characterized by intricate carvings and structural extensions.

In later times under different rulers including Mughals the Mahakaleshwar temple underwent destruction & repair, of course no harm came to Mahakal Shivling, it was only the temple building which suffered. Efforts are continuously being made to restore and preserve the cultural and religious significance of the temple. Today Mahakaleshwar temple is a revered site that symbolizes the timeless presence of Lord Shiva in the form of self-manifesting Mahakaleshwar Lingam, who is worshipped as the Lord of time and death.

The Mahakaleshwar temple has 5 floors. Lord Mahakal himself is virajit (sits) in Pataal i.e. the underground or the basement level, then is the Omkareshwar Mahadev then on the next level is a shivlinga as it is said that no one should step on the mastak (head) of Lord Mahakal himself. The upper level is Someshwar Mahadev where Naag Chandreshwar Mahadev sits & then is the main shikhar.

The architecture of the building, a blend of advanced ancient Indian science and culture was planned in such a way that when sun rose the first rays from the east would fall on Adi jaladhari as if Sun God himself was performing Mahakal's Abhishek with his radiance. When it descended towards the western horizon, its receding rays would again touch Mahakal as if seeking permission to give way to night. But today exhausts fans & walls of other temples in the premises have interfered with the celestial miracle to happen.

Often referred to as the Greenwich of India, Ujjain occupies a geographical position where the Madhyarekha (Prime Meridian of ancient India) intersects with the Karkrekha (Tropic of Cancer). The city's religious landmarks are frequently intertwined with the concept of time. This astronomical alignment emphasizes the significance of Mahakaleshwar temple dedicated to Lord Mahakal the divine embodiment that governs time.

Ever since the time when Ujjain was Avantika Van where only Gods, Rishi munis (sages) and animals dwelt, Mahakal has relieved many cursed rishi munis with his blessings. Mahakeshwar temple thus occupies a highly revered and sacred place in the hearts of innumerable devotees. It is supposed to have a pinch more virtue than all the religious places combined together.

During my stays in Avantika I felt that even an atheist if he/ she is in Avantika (present day Ujjain) for 3-4 days would turn into a theist, such is the ambience of the place and such is the power of Mahakal. Putting it simply - in Ujjain's heart, a temple stands tall, where Mahakal's sacred name echoes through ages, a temple which is so grand, where devotion's flame, it's a temple of faith and a heaven of peace.

Kishan Pandey

24 years, Ujjain.

"I feel happy in pooja path (worship) and related rituals as it creates positive vibrations within me. I was always happy in this so in spite of doing MCA I have chosen this path. For me Bhakti should be "Nischal" there should not be any bargain like - God if you do this for me I will offer 1000rs or 1 kg ladoo bhog or things like that. It should be instead that one should pray to God to just give His blessings, if His blessings are there then automatically everything good will happen to you. If I come to Mahakal and say please give me this then one day He will say that you come daily not for my darshan but only to ask for something. So don't be greedy. Mahakal's blessings are all we need.

Shiva always lives in happiness mode and that is what we need to imbibe from Him, to be happy from inside no matter how much difficulty we are facing. Time never remains the same. A smiling face will draw all negativity away sooner or later. Whenever I see Mahakal Baba I always get a feeling of happiness and a smile on my face."

Dinesh Rao

Hajipur, Bihar

"I have been visiting Mahakal since 2016. When I face Mahakal it's a different feeling altogether. He is larger than life and I felt like a miniscule in front of Mahakal Baba. The brilliance and the power of Mahakal is beyond this universe. He can make anything happen. He has the power to change you. In fact, I have felt the changes in me after Baba's darshan. Bhakti is nothing but faith in yourself and faith in your revered deity. Bhakti comes from within and cannot be forced on anyone. I feel Mahakal tells us to stay calm despite adverse situations".

CHAPTER 6

The Priests of Mahakal

Vansh Parampara

In conversation with Mahesh Pujari ji

The tradition of worshipping Mahakal has been passed down through generations since the time of Adi Shankaracharya, marking a lineage known as Vansh Parampara among the Shri Gaud Juna Brahmin families. These families hold ancient records dating back nearly 2500 years, including Tamrpatra (copper plates), Pramanpatra (documents) bestowed by Shankracharya, and sanads (royal decrees) granted by Hindu and Mughal rulers. According to these records, the Shri Gaud Juna Brahmin families have been recognized as the sole pujaris (priests) entrusted with the responsibility of conducting rituals at the Mahakaleshwar temple.

The Sri Gaud Juna Brahmin family is divided into the Khootpaati lineage comprising six families, led by Mahesh Pujari Ji and the Janeopaati lineage consisting of ten families under Pujari Vijay Shankar Ji and Pujari Surendra Sharma Ji.

These pujari families historically received all chadava (donations) made to the temple for their sustenance. Some rulers even permitted them to levy a nominal tax from every household and collect ghee for the Akhand Jyot (perpetual lamp) of Mahakal (as is evident from various sanads and documents). Exclusive rights were granted to these families to perform poojas (worship) and accept offerings from devotees. There used to be 3 patth with 3 gaddis one each for a priest from these three families where they use to sit after entering the temple, perform rituals on behalf of the devotees, give them blessings and looked after the safety and security of Baba Mahakal which continues till date. In 1971, the government took over the control of the temple, resulting in significant changes. Presently, the vansh pujaris receive 35% of the total chadava (donations) collected from the garbh graha and nandi hall of the temple. Additionally, a pujari from the Nirvani Akhada performs the bhasma snan (sacred ash bath) of Baba Mahakal daily for five minutes and is provided with sustenance in the form of food & lodging.

Another category of priests were those appointed by the Kings as their personal Brahmins who would offer prayers to Lord Mahakal on their behalf. For this service the Brahmin would get Nemnuk, Okaaf or khairat. Despite the passage of time this tradition prevails. The only change is that after the kingship ended personal Brahmins came to be appointed by the government of Madhya Pradesh instead.

Thus the third category of priests comprises individuals appointed by the government, who perform 1 pooja (prayer) & 3 aartis (except for the Bhasma Aarti & Shayan Aarti). They also perform pooja on occasions such as Shivratri, The Royal Procession in Shravan month, etc. but the exclusive right to do the shringaar (decorating and giving a form) of Mahakal remains with the Khootpaati & Janeopaati pujaris. The idols decorated on Shivratri & their staphna (installation) is also done solely by the vansh pujaris. In fact, even the ornament kaksha (room) in the Mahakal premises is opened under the supervision of 2-3 vansh pujaris -the Khootpaati & Janeopaati pujaris. The bhang shringaar, chandan shringaar, meva shringaar and all other shringaars are done only by these vansh pujaris. Morning to night most part of the rituals related to Baba Mahakal are performed by the vansh pujaris while some rituals are carried out by other category pujaris only for short durations as their duties keep changing. Unlike the vansh parampara pujaris, these government appointed pujaris receive a salary from the government for their services to Mahakaleshwar temple.

This delineation highlights the traditional lineage and the evolving administrative structure of priests at the Mahakaleshwar temple, reflecting both historical continuity and contemporary governance.

Whenever I was at Mahakaleshwar temple I could see that the Pujaris of Mahakal are so devout and true, performing the rituals with full devotion. All day long they chant and pray to Lord Mahakal with folded hands; tending to the jyotirlinga with gentle care and preparing the offerings, doing the shringaar, chanting the hymns and aartis with reverence and faith. It was as if they had dedicated their entire being to Lord Mahakal and his seva (service).

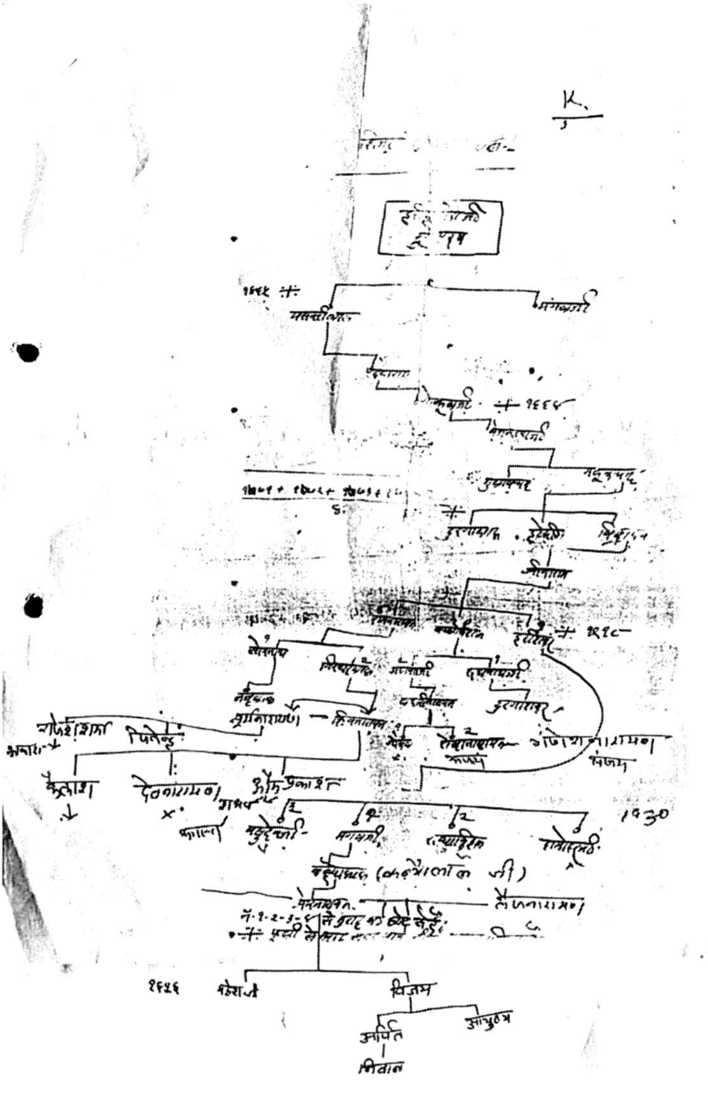

Copy of Original Vanshavalli (family history) of Khootpaati Vansh Pujaris

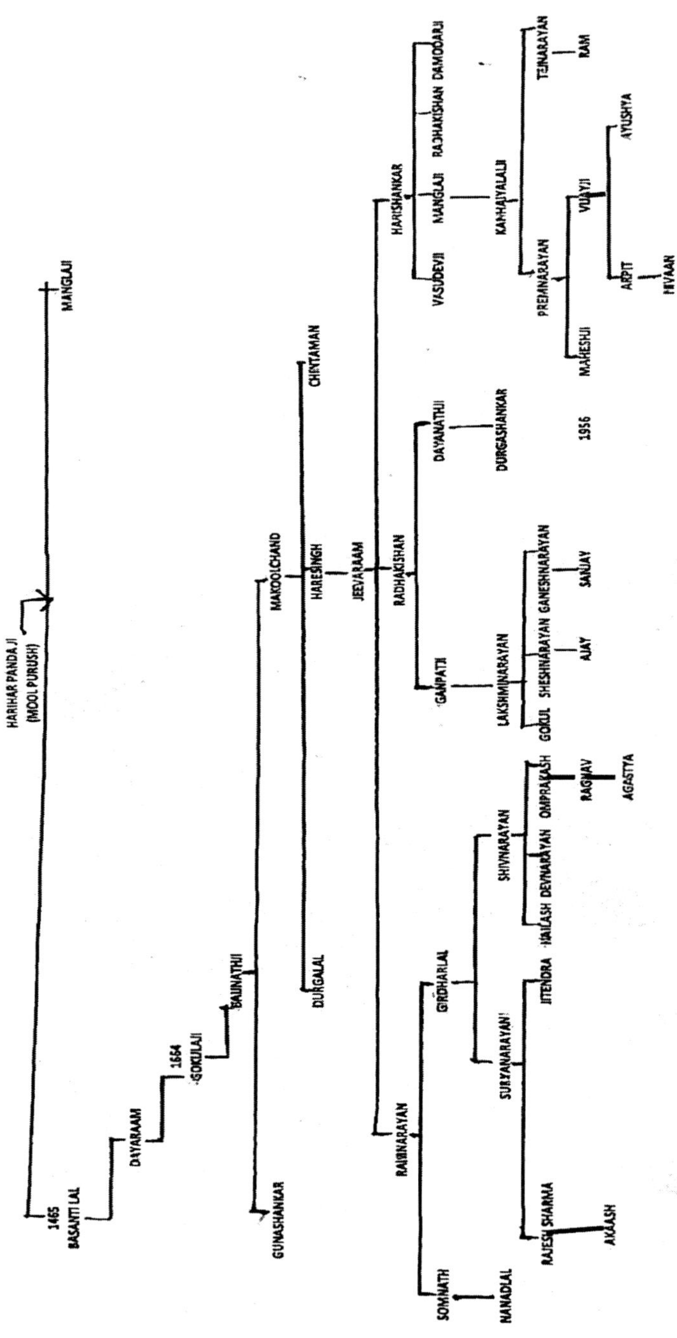
HARIHAR PANDA JI
(MOOL PURUSH)
MANGLAJI
1465
BASANTI LAL
DAYARAAM
1564
GOKULAJI
BAIJNATHJI
GUNASHANKAR
MAKOOLCHAND
CHINTAMAN
HARESINGH
DURGALAL
JEEVARAAM
HARISHANKAR
RADHAKISHAN
RAMNARAYAN
VASUDEVJI
MANGLAJI
RADHAKISHAN
DAMODARJI
KANHAIYALALJI
TEJNARAYAN
RAM
PREMNARAYAN
VIJAYJI
AYUSHYA
ARPIT
NIVAAN
MAHESHJI
1956
DAYANATHJI
DURGASHANKAR
GANPATJI
LAKSHMINARAYAN
GOKUL
SHESHNARAYAN
GANESHNARAYAN
AJAY
SANJAY
GIRDHARLAL
SHIVNARAYAN
KAILASH
DEVNARAYAN
OMPRAKASH
RAGHAV
AGASTYA
SURYANARAYAN
JITENDRA
RAJESH SHARMA
AKAASH
SOMNATH
NANADLAL

हिजरी सन् १०६१ की एक घटना है। महाकालेश्वर के तत्कालीन पुजारी ब्राह्मण ने अनेक शासकों की सनदों, प्रमाण-पत्रों के साथ तत्कालीन सम्राट् आलमगीर के निकट निवेदन किया कि महाकालेश्वर मन्दिर में नंदादीपक जलाने के लिये पिछले शासकों की आज्ञानुसार व्यय प्राप्त होता रहा है। इसलिये उन सम्राटों के आज्ञापत्रों के अनुसार ही आपके शासन से भी उस परम्परा का पोषण-समर्थन किया जाना चाहिये। इस निवेदन पर सम्राट् 'वाकयानवीस' हकीम मुहम्मद मेंहदी ने ब्राह्मणों के निकट की सनदों की जाँच-पड़ताल की और सही पाकर उस समय की तस्दीक करदी। सम्राट् आलमगीर ने अपने अधिकारी के समर्थन पर ४ सेर घी रोजाना नन्दादीप (महाकालेश्वर मंदिर में) जलाने के लिए स्वीकृत किया। यह सनद मुस्लिम सम्राट् की परधर्मसहिष्णुता का एक आदर्श उदाहरण है। इस सनद का मूल पाठ इस प्रकार है:—

शराबखते सदारत बय अलीपनाह
फजीलत व हिकमत दस्तगाह आंके
दाखिले वाके अनुमायन्द

× × ×

चार आसार वने अकबरी योमिया

तेहरीर १७ माह फरवरी इलाही सन् ७ मुआफिक तारीख ४ शव्वाल।

उक्त सनदों के अनुसार ही एक और सनद बादशाह गौरीशाह की है। यह पुजारी श्रीगोड़ जूने बसन्तलाल ब्रह्मशुक्ल उपाध्या कोटितीर्थ पर रहनेवाले को महाकालेश्वर के दर्शन कराने पर पुश्त दर पुश्त के अनुसार महाकालेश्वर की भेंट लेने, और हर घर से एक रुपया लेते रहने के लिये दी गई है। यह सनद भी उज्जैन में लिखी गई है और इसके लेखक वजीर अलीमुहम्मद हैं और मुन्शी अमीरखाँ फागुन वद्य १४ संवत् १४६५ हैं, जिसके नीचे हिन्दी में वजीर रामचरण के भी हस्ताक्षर हैं। (यह संनद बसंतलाल ब्राह्मण के वंशज श्री लक्ष्मी-नारायणजी पुजारी शनीमहाराज मन्दिरवालों के पास मौजूद है।)

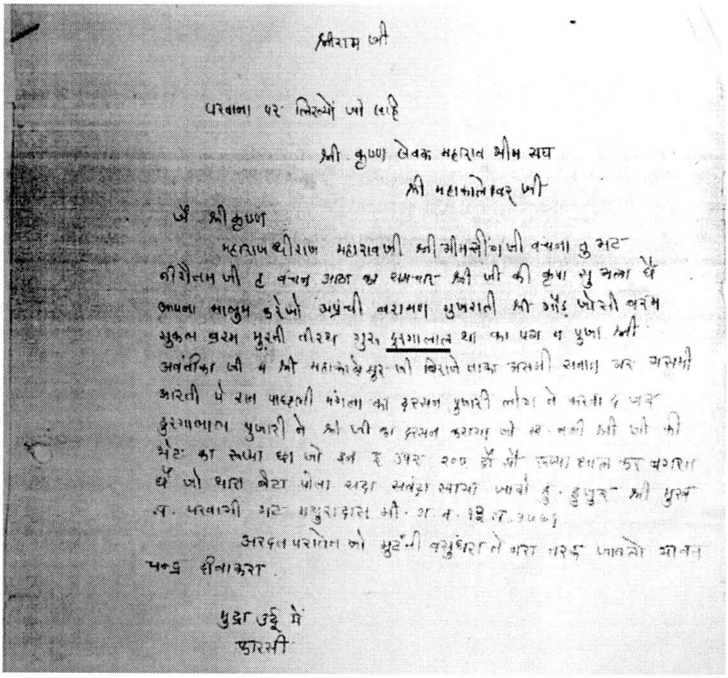

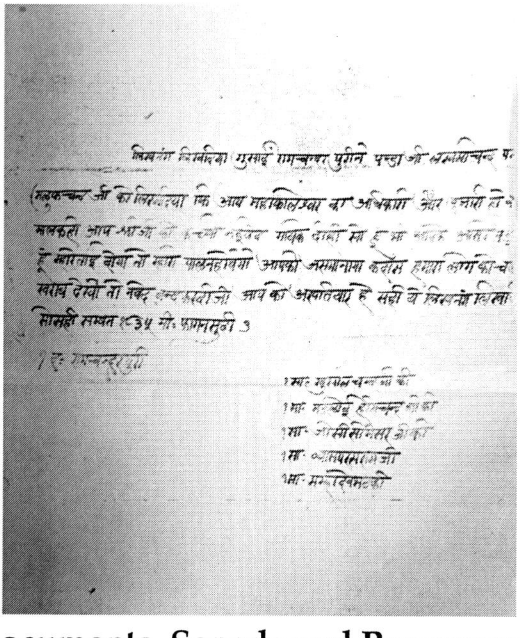

Documents, Sanads and Pramanpatras

CHAPTER 7

The Rituals and Traditions of Mahakal's Worship (Pooja Padati)

In the words of Mahesh Pujari Ji:

Mahakal's poojas (prayers) unfold daily from 4 am to 11 pm, encompassing rituals known as Utthan or jagran (awakening) and Shayan (rest). These rituals comprise of distinct poojas, evoked with 16 mantras deeply significant to devotees seeking the divine blessings of Lord Mahakal.

Each morning begins with the revered two hour Bhasma Aarti or Mangla Aarti at 4 am, a moment eagerly anticipated by devotees for its auspicious darshan.

At 7 am, the second aarti "Karpur Gauram Karunavtaaram..." commences with the offering of Baal Bhog, consisting of rice and curd to Mahakal.

The 10 am aarti "Karpur Gauram Karunavtaaram....." is accompanied by a complete meal including rice, dal, vegetables, ghee, curd, and roti, offered to Mahakal in his Nirakaar roop devoid of ornaments or any defined form.

After the 5 pm panchamrita poojan with 5 mantras, jalabhisekh stops marking the transition to Mahakal's Saakar roop from Nirakaar roop, adorned and decorated (shringarit roop) with chandan(sandal), bhang, meva(dry fruits) etc. for devotees to behold until 11 pm.

During the 7 pm aarti "Jai mangal murti shiv mangal murti..., cow milk is offered to Lord Mahakal.

The day culminates with the Shayan aarti "Om jai shiv onkara.... at 10:30 pm, where another sumptuous meal is offered to Baba Mahakal before he retires for the night.

There are two akhand jyotis (silver lamps in which sacred flame glows continuously of 11 cotton wicks each) known as "Nanda deepak "in the grabha griha (sanctum sanctorum)one is lit with ghee dedicated to Lord Shiva while the other is lit with mustard oil for Parvati i.e. Shakti. In the past the ghee and oil was provided by the priests, the kings or the devotees, but currently this is being taken care of by the Mahakaleshwar temple Committee also.

Each of these prayers and aartis unfold with meticulous reverence amidst mantra chanting & drum beats, offering the devotees a profound and transformative spiritual experience, especially during Mahakal's adorned Saakar forms, which vary each time, adding to the divine spectacle.

It is an out of this world experience to witness any or all of these.

The Mahakal Shiv Linga

According to Mahesh Pujari ji "All lingas are manifestations of the soul (aatma lingas), representing the essence of Shiva in the form of jyoti (light). Shivalinga manifests spontaneously in the form of this divine light and then takes a tangible form, such as stone or ice (as in the case of the Amarnath Shiv linga), over countless years, dating back to the Satyuga era."

As per beliefs the Mahakal Shivlinga manifested with the creation of Earth itself being the oldest Shivlinga of the world first in the form of a jyoti (light) then taking a solid form.

Pujari Akash Sharma

Mahakaleshwar Temple, Ujjain.

"I feel bhakti is what gives us peace. And the most important lesson we can learn from Shiva is how to take everyone along together like Shiva has Vasuki snake as well as Nandi bull both are enemies but HE keeps them together. Same way, in today's times we should learn to maintain and keep our relations harmoniously & Meditation is something all age groups can learn from The Adiyogi Shiva."

G. Mishra

Real Estate Business.

"When I was a kid I had read about Mahakal. It could be because in my family, we worship Lord Shiva. So, from childhood, we have been devoted to the worship of Shiva. So in 2008 I visited Mahakal. I went there as a devotee, meaning I wanted to have the darshan of Baba and receive his blessings. That was my purpose for going there. When I went there, a friend accompanied me. My experience with him was such that my friend used to experience some kind of negative energy. During the Bhasma Aarti, he started crying very loudly and intensely. I held his hand, and when the Aarti was over, he was completely silent and calm. This was the first time we went, and since then, he has never felt any negative energy. He has visited Mahakal two or three times ever since. This is the power of the Bhasma Aarti and of Mahakal. When you are in front of Baba you get goosebumps. All the negative thoughts and processes that come to your mind, all of that negativity ends with the Bhasma Aarti as if you yourself have taken a sacred bath. There is tremendous energy there that you can feel. It is something you cannot express in words. You can feel it when you are with Mahakal.

I feel Shiva teaches us to lead a simple life with high thinking and to help everyone. Shiva has everything; he is Mahadev, the greatest of gods, and he gives to everyone - to gods, to humans, and even to nature. Nature is Shiva and Shiva is nature."

CHAPTER 8

Mahakal's Bhasma Aarti

Believe me when I say that being present in the two hour long sacred ritual of Bhasma Aarti of Mahakal has the power to transform you at a fundamental level from the core. It can change your entire DNA not physically but spiritually, yes. Consider yourself fortunate and chosen by the divine if you have had the privilege to sit through this sacred ritual. It's an awareness that can redefine your entire existence—I speak from personal experience, having been blessed to attend two Bhasma Aartis, including one where I sat in the Nandi Mandapam (hall) right in front of the majestic Mahakal.

Before I share my experience, let me first describe the Aarti itself as briefed by Mahesh Pujari ji along with my personal observation.

The Brahma muhurat Bhasma Aarti or the Mangla aarti is more than just a ritual; it is a breathtaking spectacle that immerses you in profound devotion and spirituality.

For centuries, the tradition of applying bhasma to Lord Shiva has been upheld, rooted in several mythological stories. Legend has it that when Sati's father insulted Lord Shiva, she entered the yagya vedi (sacred fire) in anger. Overcome with grief, Lord Shiva wandered with her body, causing disruption across the three worlds. To calm him, Lord Vishnu intervened, using his Sudarshan chakra (spinning disc like weapon) to sever Sati's body into many khands (pieces) of which 51 exist in India now. The remnants of her body became sacred places known as Shaktipeeths, with only Sati's ash left with Shiva. In his sorrow, Lord Shiva applied the bhasma (ash) all over his body, symbolizing his refusal to be parted from his beloved wife Sati. This tradition continues today, where Lord Shiva is revered with offerings of bhasma (but in a different form).

Mahakal alone is adorned with ash; no other form or jyotirlinga of Shiva is adorned with ash.

The Mangla Aarti or commonly known as the Bhasma Aarti commences at around 4 am with a solemn invocation to Veerbhadra, a fierce form of Lord Shiva and a bell being rung after which the silver gate is opened and the pujaris and sevaks (caretakers) go inside for meticulous cleaning of the garbha griha and the entire precinct is purified and pujaris do a small kapoor aarti. With the ringing of another bell exactly at 4 am, devotees, who have patiently queued since midnight (without their mobile phones), are ushered in through various mandapas (halls) i.e. the Nandi Mandapam, Ganpati Mandapam and Kartikey Mandapam. The inner sanctum or the garbha griha has been for a few years now inaccessible to the general public due to overwhelming crowds.

The steadfast devotion of the devotees is rewarded as they catch the first glimpse of their revered deity, Mahakal.

The rituals continue with jalabhishek, where water from Kotiteerth (the sacred kund with the water of all sacred rivers of Akhand Bharat) sanctifies Mahakal. According to Indian mythology Lord Hanuman was carrying the water of all the sacred rivers of Akhand Bharat for Lord Ram's Rajyaabhisekh (coronation ceremony). He rested here for Mahakal's darshan and as the pot was full and Lord Hanuman could not accumulate the water of the pond in that pot, hearing Akashvani (voice from heaven) Lord Hanumaan emptied the pot in this Kund (pond) and ones the water mixed with Kotikund water, Hanumanji refilled the pot, since then called the Kotiteerth. There is a temple of Lord Hanuman near the Koti teerth called Suryamukhi Hanuman temple where Lord Hanumaan is seen with a water pot. As per Mahesh guruji legend has it that there are two more water kunds deep below the Kotiteerth called kund and kundiya. It is believed that in the big Kund(pond) Lord Bholenath used to bathe and with the water of the Kundiya Goddess Parvati use to take bath, as such Koti teerth pond is considered a very pious one.

All this while mantras resonate through the air, creating a spiritual atmosphere.

In the ethereal ambiance of the Bhasma Aarti, the divine scene unfolds with intricate rituals. Behind Mahakal, Goddess Parvati is meticulously adorned with 16 shringaar as befitting a wedded lady, vibrant clothes and fragrant garlands. At the same time Lord Ganesh and Lord Kartikeya present on either sides inside the garbha griha are also adorned and worshipped. Nandi is embellished in resplendent garments, and an earthen lamp glows beside him, honoring the provision of Gana (companions/ attendants of Shiva) pooja.

After the jalabhisekh, Mahakal is bathed with milk, curd, sugar, honey, ghee, (known as the panchamrit poojan) further enriched with sugandh (aroma) like kesar (saffron), itra (perfume), vijaya (bhang), and fruit juice with 16 mantras after which Mahakal ones again is bathed with Harihar jal (water) from the koti teerth and the entire jaladhari is cleaned and purified allowing for Mahakal's shringaar. It is unbelievable but as per the pujaris they never have a set pattern for the shringaar of Mahakal, they just start adorning HIM and are literally guided by Mahakal to take the form HE desires.

Women devotees respectfully veil their eyes as Mahakal undergoes the sanctifying Bhasma snan, a ritual bath of Mahakal in Nirakaar swaroop symbolizing purity and devotion. A sant (saint) from Maha Nirvani Akhada reverently performs this act for a mere five minutes before retreating, ensuring the sanctity of the ceremony.

The ash used in this ritual holds profound significance. According to Mahesh Pujariji it is not ordinary cremation ash, as "no human remains are pure enough to be offered to Shiva. Only the ash of Goddess Sati, who attained Shiva through intense penance, was considered pure for Shiva". The ash used for Mahakal's bhasma snan is prepared from the uple (cake like compressed structure made from cowdung) of Kapila cows blended with sacred components from the Shami, Palash, Ber, Peepal, and Banyan trees. This mixture is carefully dried, sieved, and then encased in a white cloth potli (bundle). The entire preparation unfolds in a dedicated room within the temple precincts, reserved exclusively for this sacred purpose.

During the divine ritual of Bhasma snan, Mahakal is first covered with a white cloth, a symbolic act of purity and reverence so that his shringarit roop(adorned form) doesn't get distorted. This cloth is then removed for the subsequent bath with Bhasma as a symbolic form, signifying the direct communion between the deity and the sacred ashes. The removal of the cloth marks the transition into a deeper spiritual connection during the ritual.

The Bhasma snan of Mahakal though brief, resonates deeply, evoking transformation and reverence among all who witness its sanctified moments.

Following the Bhasma snan, Mahakal is adorned with ornaments, garlands, etc. Navaidya (sacred food) is placed before Mahakal as the morning offering. He is then worshipped with dhoop (incense), deep (lighted lamp) and Naivedya. Any bhet (offerings) from devotees in the form of money, clothes and a variety of items such as dry fruits, ladoos, fruits, jewellery like Mukut (crown), etc is offered to Baba Mahakal. These offerings are made amidst the melodious chanting of mantras and shlokas, invoking divine blessings upon the gathered devotees.

After the offerings (bhet), the aarti "Jai mangal murti shiv mangal murti......" is sung. Then mantra Pushpanjali is chanted with shama yachna (forgiveness from Lord Mahakal for any error in performing the sacred rituals).

The rhythmic beats of drums, manjiras, and ghantis fill the air, resonant chants of "Har Har Mahadev" and "Jai Mahakal" echo passionately from the devotees. The atmosphere becomes charged with devotion and spiritual fervor, culminating in a profound moment when the lights are turned off for a few minutes during the aarti. In this momentary darkness, only Mahakal's divine form illuminated by the aarti's flames remains visible. After this sankalp is recited that the first pooja (prayer) of the day has been performed.

That brings to the poorna samapan (completion) of the Bhasma Aarti.

At the conclusion of the Bhasma Aarti, the pujaris recite a mantra dedicated to Nandi, the supreme devotee of Lord Shiva, honoring his steadfast devotion and service along with the other ganas ((companions/attendants) of Shiva.

"वान रावण चंडी नंदी भिरंगी जटाधारो सदा शिव प्रसादेन सर्वे गंधंतुशम्भवा"

"Vaan ravana chandi nandi bhirngi jatadharo sada shiv prasaden sarve gandhantushambhava"

Aarti, ghanti, jhanjh, damru, nandi, etc all are worshipped and their names are taken as no prayer to Shiva is considered complete without prayer to his ganas who are loved by Him.

As for me it was at the juncture when the lights were turned off momentarily during the Bhasma aarti that a profound transformation occurred within my heart. Emotions overflew, shivers ran through my entire body, tears flowed, and a sense of ecstasy enveloped my soul. In this transcendent moment, the boundary between the devotee and the divine dissolves, leaving only the pure realization that nothing exists except Mahakal. I felt like Mahakal was watching me in real....that HE was actually in front of me. I couldn't bulge or even think of seeing anything or anyone around me as if I was glued to the larger than life vision of Mahakal. Time appeared to stand still, stretching into eternity as I gazed upon the majestic manifestation of Mahakal, my entire being suspended in a moment of awe allowing me to behold the divine form in all its glory. Later I recalled it was something like we saw in the Mahabharat serial when everything came to a halt on Krishna adorning his original form in front of Arjuna to give him Geeta Updesh (sermon). Same was what I felt, my eyes all wide open as if to take in each moment of my personal contact and a deep sense of connection with Mahakal. It is an experience beyond words, where I felt and understood the ultimate joy. I was no longer bound by the constraints of my own identity and was instead fully immersed in the experience. The emotions that arose were overwhelming as I underwent a deep sense of bliss enveloping my soul and filling me with a sense of pure awareness.

In those fleeting moments of subtle yet radiant awareness I felt a profound sense of peace and understanding that spoke volumes to my heart whispering secrets to my soul leaving me humble.

This ritualistic journey through devotion and divine communion left an indelible imprint on not only me, but all those fortunate enough to participate in the Bhasma Aarti, guiding them closer to the ultimate truth and bliss of Mahakal's presence.

Nothing is there ...only Mahakal.....we are nothing, zero....

You have to be a part of it to feel the ULTIMATE joy ....

:शिवाय ।। ।। जय महाकाल ।। ।। ॐ नमः शि

।। महाकालेश्वर भगवान की आरती ।।

ॐ जय मंगलमूर्ति, शिव मंगलमूर्ति,
दर्शनमात्रेमन स्मरण मात्रेमन, कामनापूर्ति, ॐ जयदेव जयदेव ।।
अहो सुखकर्ता, दुखहर्ता, वार्ता विघ्नाची, अहो वार्ता विघ्नाची,
नुरवी पुरवी प्रेम, नुरवी पुरवी प्रेम, कृपा जयांची (दिवान्दी)
अहो सर्वांगी सुन्दर, उटी शेंदुराची अहो मध्ये नवराशी,
कंठी झलके माल, कंठी शोभे माल, मुक्ता फलांची । ॐ जयदेव जयदेव ।।
जय मंगलमूर्ति अहो शिव मंगलमूर्ति, दर्शनमाझेमन,
स्मरण मात्रेमन, कामनमूर्ति ॐ जयदेव जयदेव,
अहो रत्न खचिंत पत्रा, तुंज गौरी कुमारा, अहो तुज गौरी कुमारा,
चन्दनाची उटी सिंदूराची उटी कुंकुम केशरा ।
अहो हीरे जड़ित मुगुट शौभेतो बरा, अहो शौभेतो बरा
रुण झुणती नुपुरे रुण झुणती नुपुरे चरणो घांगरिया ॐ जयदेव जयदेव ।।
जय मंगलमूर्ति, अहो शिव मंगलमूर्ति दर्शन मात्रेमन,
स्मरण मात्रेमन, कामना पुरती ॐ जयदेव जयदेव ।। 2 ।।
अहो लम्बोदर पीताम्बर फणीवर वंदना अहो फणिवर वंदना
सरल सोइ वक्र तुंड त्रिनयना, अहो वक्र, तुंड त्रिनयना,
अहो दास रामचा, वाट पाहे सदना, अहो वाट पाहे सदना,
संकष्टी पावावै, निर्वाणी रक्षावें, सुरवर गजवंदना । ॐ जयदेव जयदेव
जय मंगलमूर्ति अंहो शिव मंगलमूर्ति दर्शन मात्रेमन
जय मंगलमूर्ति, अहो शिव मंगलमूर्ति दर्शन मात्रेमन,
स्मरण मात्रेमन, कामना पुरती ॐ जयदेव जयदेव ।। 3 ।।
अहो लवथवती विक्राल ब्रह्माण्डी माला अहो ब्रह्माण्डी माला
विषे कण्ठे काला, विषे कण्डे काला त्रिनेत्री ज्वाला,
अहो लावण्ये सुन्दर मस्तकी भाला अहो मस्तकी भाला तेथुनियाजल निर्मल
तेथुनियाजल निर्मल बाहे झुलझुला ॐ जयदेव जयदेव ।
जय शिवशंकरा, अहो स्वामी शंकरा, आरतीं औवालूं,
भावार्थी औवालूं, तुज कर्पूर गौरा ॐ जयदेव जयदेव ।।4 ।।
अहो व्याघ्राम्बर फणिवर, सुन्दर मदनारी, अहो सुन्दर मदनारी
पचानन मनमोहन, पचानन मनमोहन, मुनिजन सुखकारी
अहो शतकोटिचे बीज, वाचे उच्चारी, अहो वाचे उच्चारी रघुकुल तिलकराम
रघुकुल तिलकाराम दासा अन्तरी । ॐ जयदेव जयदेव ।।
ॐ जय शिवशंकरा, अहो स्वामी शंकरा, आरतीं औवालूं,
भावार्थी औवालूं, तुज कर्पूर गौरा ॐ जयदेव जयदेव ।।4 ।।

Jai mangal murti shiv mangal murti aarti

Vineet Singh

53 years, Mumbai

"I hold a strong belief in a higher power that governs the universe and humanity's place within it.

To me Bhakti is surrender. It allows you to release the burden of control & focus on personal growth. You accept your current situation but strive to become a better version of yourself.

Every heartbeat, every breath is a reminder of the Divine."

Rahul Rajput

25 years, travel blogger & photographer.

"Mahakal is everything to me. Whenever I go there I get strength to face the world .There is a flow of energy in Mahakal Baba that you can only feel. I feel today's generation sees that Shiva consumes bhang but what they overlook is the reason why Shiva did that. He even consumed poison. Do we have the capacity to do that? No, then we should not take things in a negative sense rather Shiva teaches to stop showing off. He has everything yet He lives a simple life. He tells us to meditate and grow our mental strength."

CHAPTER 9

Mahakal: Festivals and Sacred Observances

Shivratri

During Shivratri, a sacred festival transformed into Shiv Navratri or the nine nights of Lord Shiva starting from Panchmi date at the abode of Mahakal, the celestial rituals unfold with mystical grandeur. Eleven appointed pujaris of the government perform the Laghurudra abhishek from 9 am to 12 noon, an intricate ceremony invoking divine blessings, where each day of the nine-day celebration reveals a different manifestation of Mahakal, each one more amazing and awe-inspiring than the other.

The inaugural day adorns Mahakal with chandan, bhang, shola and bhambhar symbolizing purity and devotion. Second day Mahakal is adorned with Sheshnaag along with shola and bhambhar. Next He manifests His form as Ghatatop. Following day along with Sheshnaag and ghatatop a shiv pratima mukhota (face) of silver is placed giving his devotees His Chabina darshan. On the next day Mahakal manifests in his Holkar swaroop with the following day being adorned as Manmahesh sitting on a chowki. 7th day Mahakal is in His Uma Mahesh manifestation. The 8th day devotees witness Mahakal in His Shiv tandav roop. On the auspicious day of Shivratri, Mahakal assumes the formless Nirakaar swaroop, embodying transcendence beyond human perception, jalabhisekh being done the entire day. Before shivratri from midnight to 4 am Mahapooja, panchamritt poojan and abhisekh is performed. After abhisekh saptdhatu mukhota (idol made of seven metals) is placed on Mahakal & offered with 1008 names shivnamavali bilvapatra followed by 7 dhan (grains) amounting to 101 kg being offered on Mahakal's idol with the chanting of 7 khadya mantras. Post the meticulous four-prahar pooja, Mahakal transforms into the majestic Bridegroom, adorned with a magnificent floral sehra (face cover made of flowers) and a garland of kankan, a sight known as "Sehra Darshan". This sacred ritual unfolds from the early hours until noon, drawing devotees into a profound communion with the divine. At noon, the Sehra Darshan concludes, marking the singular occasion when Bhasma Aarti is performed in the afternoon, a rare departure from its customary dawn timing.

Mahesh guruji enlightened not only me but I feel many readers will benefit knowing that if a person is not able to offer much or anything to Mahakal/Shiva, he can just do the Manas pooja by reciting the 5 shlokas of Manas pooja (mentioned in Shiv Sagar) which will amount to the devotee offering everything be it belpatra, ornaments, sweets, money etc. to Lord Shiva.

The Royal Procession of Mahakal

During Shravan month (as per Hindu calendar), the sovereign Mahakal, revered as the King of Ujjain, embarks on a regal procession from 4 pm to 7 pm. Enshrined in a silver palanquin, adorned in Saakar swaroop, he tours the city to commune with his subjects. Symbolically, a linga consecrated during pranpratishta assumes its place within the palanquin, symbolizing divine presence among the people. This royal procession occurs every

Monday through Shravan and sometimes even in Bhado month (the number of processions vary as per certain rules and rituals).

I was blessed to be a part of one royal procession. Post noon devotees had started gathering for a mere glimpse of their much-loved Raja Mahakal alongside the path(road) he was to take. They were standing atop scooters, perched on trees, on various shops (in fact I myself was so engrossed in the euphoria that I too had climbed on top of a shop counter and well nobody says no at that time), anywhere from where they could get a close glimpse of Mahakal raja. Flowers were being distributed by almost anyone to shower on "The Maharaja" when His royal chariot came. In the temple premises from 3 pm onwards the symbolic Mahakal is adorned and worshipped first at the sabha mandap before placing him in a silver paalki(palanquin) befitting a King. When his paalki comes out of the temple sharp at 4pm he is given a guard of honour. A police contingent playing the band moves in front .Then comes various bands, damru players, dancers etc. with Shiv bhajans by different Mandalis. His paalki is followed by a different Rath (chariot) every time and then a form (roop) of Mahakal riding on an elephant as befitting a Maharaja moves along. High ranking Police officials and other high profile dignitaries all feel like sevaks(caretaker) and are always more than willing to be a part of the procession and King Mahakal's safety.

Each Savari (royal procession) adds on a form (swaroop) of Mahakal, the first savari having one, the second having two forms of Mahakal one in silver palanquin and one in a Ratha. Third savari sees three forms and so on.

A mere glimpse and the loud chants of "Jai Mahakal", "Jai raja Mahakal", "Har Har Mahadev" from the devotees are enough to send shivers up your spine. The voice coming from thousands of devotees is so loud that even the best of loudspeakers would fail, in fact I felt like I was being transported to the times where grand royal processions used to take place. Actually in those moments I felt like I was a commoner waiting to lie down on the path of my beloved King. Such is the atmosphere. The damru sounds, the nagadas, the devotional songs, the Har Har Mahadev chants of the devotees are enough to make even the so-called modern youngsters be a part of this spiritual moment. Yes people of all age groups from few month old kids to 80+ elderly people all felt united like one big family under their beloved King Mahakal during that time. And with every Royal procession the fervor keeps going up year after year. The savaari returns with the same ambience and devotional fervor to the temple exactly at 7 pm as Lord Mahakal is believed to be on fast every Monday of Shravan month and at 7pm aarti he opens his day long fast.

These sacred traditions not only enrich the spiritual tapestry of Ujjain but also beckon devotees to partake in the timeless rituals that honour Mahakal, the eternal guardian and embodiment of cosmic grace signifying a sacred ritual of our ancient culture.

Harihar Bhet

On the auspicious day of Vaikuntha Chaturdashi in Kartik month (according to Indian calendar), Ujjain resonates with the mystical harmony of Hari-Har Milan at the Gopala Temple. According to mythological beliefs, during the Chaturmas period, Lord Vishnu goes to rest in the Kshir Sagar (milky ocean). On Baikuntha Chaturdashi of Kartik month Lord Mahakal then hands over the responsibility of taking care of the world back to Lord Vishnu, an occasion of celestial festivity. Worship of Lord Shiva and Vishnu is performed together, known as Hari-Har Milan (union of Lord Vishnu and Shiva). 'Hari' refers to Lord Vishnu and 'Hara' refers to Lord Shiva. This Harihar bhet/milan is during night when Lord Mahakal emerges from his sanctum in the Mahakaleshwar Temple, carried in a majestic silver palanquin during the revered "Avantikanath" procession. The ceremony culminates with the offering of Bilva patra garlands to Lord Vishnu at the Gopala Temple and only here and on this special occasion is Mahakal offered with a Tulsi garland. After the rituals, the procession returns to Mahakaleshwar Temple, synchronizing this grand spectacle with the divine Bhasma Aarti of Mahakal. The tradition of Hari-Har Milan is mentioned in various Puranas.

Dr. Ajay Yadav
Lucknow.

"Shiva is Shaswat, Shiva is Adi, Shiva is Anant - the eternal, the original, and the infinite. To me, Shiv represents the ultimate reality that transcends birth and death, existing beyond the bounds of time and space.

I was introduced to Mahakal in my childhood through stories in Amar Chitra Katha and have been to Mahakal over 10 times, every year in the month of Shravan. Ever since I was a child, I've been captivated by the grandeur and majesty of the word 'Mahakal' itself through Amar Chitra Katha. My fascination with Mahakal has only grown stronger over time, and I find myself drawn to the sheer power and mystique surrounding this enigmatic figure.

As I reflect on the challenging time my father faced in 2014 when he suffered a severe stroke, it suddenly occurred to me that if he were to recover, I would make it a point to visit Mahakal every Shravan. Since then, I have been making it a ritual to visit Mahakal every year during the Shravan month as a way to express gratitude for my father's recovery.

The significance of Mahakal is indeed profound, and the energy it evokes is unparalleled. When I think of Mahakal, I feel a surge of confidence and faith that whatever I'm undertaking will be accomplished with His divine guidance and blessings.

When I visit Mahakal, I'm filled with a sense of lightness, a feeling of accomplishment and liberation. It's as if I've checked off all the boxes on my list, and I can finally take a deep breath and relax. The feeling is hard to put into words, but it's like I've earned a badge of honor, a symbol that I've made it through another year and can face whatever challenges come my way.

When you trust in Mahakal, transformation is inevitable. Whenever I recall Mahakal, even in the most challenging situations, I find a glimmer of hope. I may not always understand the methods used to guide me, but eventually, I discover a path forward. Remember, it's up to you to take control and fight for your path. But know that Mahakal will always be with you, providing guidance and support."

Dr. Srikant

Karnataka

"I had heard a lot about Mahakal from my North Indian friends and now I got a chance to come here. Whatever I had heard from my friends is nothing compared to what I felt after Mahakal's darshan. Being a doctor I lead a very hectic life and here I felt as if all my tiredness was gone, I felt relaxed as if a heavy load had been taken off me. I felt at peace with myself. I felt I could forever keep looking at Mahakal...the Mahakal shivlinga is actually larger than life as I felt it. There is an undefined pull and energy there which attracts you. I feel like I have got a new life .Now I can go back relaxed knowing Mahakal will take care of everything. Though it is entirely on Mahakal's will, but I will try coming again and again. I feel so blessed."

Chapter 10

Mysteries & Beliefs Surrounding Mahakal

The Mahakaleshwar temple in Ujjain is enveloped in both scientific intrigue and mythological mystique, deeply influencing its devotees.

Legend has it that no king or ruler can reside in Ujjain at night because the city belongs solely to King Mahakal as no human authority is above him. Any king defying this tradition faces dire consequences, as the saying goes, "two kings cannot live in one city." It is said that even King Vikramaditya ruled Ujjain on behalf of King Mahakal and not as King himself.

The Mahakaleshwar temple holds a unique geographical significance: the Tropic of Cancer intersects precisely at its pinnacle.

Scientists recognize the Mahakaleshwar Jyotirlinga as a focal point of energy. Positioned in an auspicious solar spot, it is believed to harness solar energies that amplify the temple's ambiance for peace and meditation.

Notably, Mahakaleshwar is the sole Dakshinmukhi (south-facing) Jyotirlinga, symbolically aligning with themes of time and mortality.

The temple's architectural layout spans five levels, including an underground chamber where it is believed that Lord Shiva performed the Tandava, the cosmic dance of creation and destruction.

There is a myth that Juna Mahakal (inside Mahakaleshwar temple premises) is the original Mahakal but the fact as told by Mahesh pujari ji is that it is Vradha Kaleshwar Mahadev. With time its name got distorted to Juna Mahakal. The myth that it is the original must have been spread to fool invaders and save the real Mahakal Shivlinga.

Mahakaleshwar temple is revered as one of the seven Mukti Sthalas, (liberation sites) where devotees believe that death and cremation lead to moksha and freedom from the cycle of rebirth.

It is believed that whatever you wish from Mahakal will be granted provided you wish with a pure heart and without any harmful intention to anyone.

The mysteries and spiritual significance associated with the Mahakaleshwar temple continue to mesmerize and ignite the curiosity of seekers of divine truth, blending ancient lore with profound cosmic symbolism.

Pt. Shreyas Chaturvedi

26 years, Mahakaleshwar temple, Ujjain.

"I have been in Mahakal baba's seva ever since I was a small kid. After I completed my graduation I started performing pooja in Mahakaleshwar temple. Right now I am doing MA in Veda from Vikram University, Ujjain.

It doesn't matter whether I am a pujari or a common person, bhakti I feel is aradhana (worship) of God through which we find our peace and this takes us towards positivity. Mahakal has a nirakaar form, he is not attached to any materialistic thing, you offer him only water and he is happy with that so if we want to be happy in every situation we need to learn this from Shiva to detach ourselves at the right time from over materialism and not have too much expectations rather do our work sincerely. Mahakal will not let your sincere efforts go to waste."

Ms. Reena Rawat

45yrs, Yoga therapist, Durgapur, WB.

"When I visited Mahakal after the darshan I felt a sense of peace and wellbeing within me. There was a sudden surge of energy in front of Mahakal Shivlinga. I felt like I was divinely charged with positivity. For me Bhakti is a spiritual path of dedication and love for the divine leading to freedom from the cycle of birth, death and rebirth.. Being a yoga therapist myself I feel that we all need to learn Yoga from the Adiyogi, Shiva. Along with yoga which helps us to be fit physically , mentally and emotionally which is the need of the day, we can learn compassion, detachment from too much materialism and most of all search for pure happiness inside ourselves instead of seeking it outside ."

CHAPTER 11

Mahakal and Samsana: An Attempt at Exploring their Sacred Bond

Does Shiva really reside in Samsana? This is really tough to know as every learned person has their own opinion about it.

There is a chapter about Devi Sati's conversation with her father Daksha about lord Shiva in Shreemad Bhagvat Purana where Sati is actually glorifying lord Shiva, by explaining the actual nature of lord Shiva unlike what Daksha thinks of.

"It's only you who thinks that he is "Ashiva" (Not pure) and nobody else, if it is true then why otherwise lord Shiva, who resides in Cremation ground (Smashana) with Bhoot-Pishachhya, Is praised by lord Brahma & other devatas (Gods) and why would Brahma and other God's would have kept the flowers fallen from his feet on their heads."

The story of Goddess Uma (Parvati) asking Shiva why he resides in Rudra bhoomi is specifically found in the Shiva Purana.

Once Goddess Uma asked Lord Shiva" Why Rudra Bhoomi? Why do you like Rudra Bhoomi?"

To which Lord Shiva replied "a human after death stays in the rudra bhoomi alone, scared, devastated and clueless. That is why I stay there too. To make sure he's not alone. To console him. To tell him that I shall give him yet another chance to gain wisdom. After all, we are 'Jagatah Pitaro Vande Parvati Parameshwara' the parents of every life in this creation. So, as the father, it is my duty to help the wounded and pained child reach me. That is why I stay at the Rudra Bhoomi."

The soul cries heart-wrenchingly, lamenting on how wasted and pointless its life has been as it had not thought of and earned the real wealth that is God's blessing and progress toward moksha. It stays in the rudra bhoomi alone, scared, devastated and clueless. That is why Shiva stays there to console and make sure it is not alone.

This is the reason Shiva in his Ansh or Rudra form resides in Samsana to be with us when all our near and dear ones leave us not even turning to look back even ones ...the reality of life. When we are alive all are around us but no sooner does our life ends and the body taken to the cremation ground, after the rituals all our near and dear ones leave not even once turning back to see if all is well with the body which is now turned to ashes...the soul (as per the Hindu scriptures) watches everyone leaving, sad and alone ... it's at this point that Shiva in the form of His Ansh or Rudra comes to the soul to lighten the deep sorrow it is feeling, to be with it and to make it feel happy on being one with Shiva even in the agony of being left by our relatives . That's the connection of Shiva with Samsana.

Shiva is telling us that, the beautiful physical body we always boast of, will turn into a pile of ash one day. So we should stop giving importance to materialistic things, and evolve above our physical self.

रुद्रकालीरदित्यश्च श्मशानेष्वविराजते ।
तत्र शम्भुः प्रसन्नात्मा विचरति न संशयः॥

"RudraKali, Aditya (Sun) shine forth in cremation grounds. There, Shambhu (Shiva), with a tranquil soul, moves around without doubt."

This verse highlights the presence of Shiva (Shambhu) in cremation grounds alongside other divine forms, emphasizing his transcendental nature and his association with places symbolizing death and transformation.

According to Mahesh Pujari ji, "during the incidence when King Daksh's head was severed and the atmosphere turned into a somber cremation ground with lifeless bodies scattered around due to Lord Shiva's anger over Sati immolating herself, Shiva later transformed the scene into a divine realm. All the deceased were revived, and Daksh himself received a goat's head transplant. This illustrates Shiva's power to convert a place of cremation into a celestial abode. Bholenath resides only in Kailash. It's his Ansh/ Rudra forms that reside in Samsana to see that nothing wrong happens there." Such an insightful interpretation.

Naga sadhu Rajesh Puri

(lives in Samshan, Ujjain)

"Mahakal sabki manokaamna poori karte hei. He is the father of the world - Jagatpita. He only calls those whom he wants to call rest no one can come for his darshan if He does not want them to. Take at least 1 hour from your 24 hour day to devote to Shiva. Do Om Namoh Shivai. I have been regularly going to Mahakal temple for the last 40 years. HE is always there. It is said that guru of Brahmin is a Sanyasi, Guru of Sanyasi is Avinashi (Shiva).But Avinashi has no guru...He is Anadi...always present...We should learn sanskaar (culture) from Shiva like our father mother teach us when we are young ...learn to give... learn to have faith...learn to control our senses.....learn Yoga... Jai baba Mahakal...Jo ek baar baba Mahakal ke paas sache dil se a gaya vo humesha unhi ki kripa drishti mei rehega (Someone who sincerely comes to Lord Mahakal will always remain under His compassionate gaze.)"

Chapter 12

Understanding Bhakti: The Essence of Devotion

As children, we looked up to our fathers as superheroes, capable of accomplishing the impossible. We felt safe in their presence, knowing they would shield us from every harm. That unwavering trust was the foundation of a parent child bond.

In a similar way, Bhakti is about surrendering to the divine, entrusting ourselves completely to the care of the supreme being. It's about recognizing that our existence is not our own, but a gift from the divine. We can close our eyes, letting go of all doubts and fears, knowing that our beloved deity is watching over us, guiding us through life's journey.

Just as our fathers would protect and provide for us, believe that the supreme power (call Him by any name) will provide for us in every way, even when we can't see the path ahead. Bhakti is that deep-seated trust that fosters a sense of safety and security, allowing us to navigate life's challenges with courage and confidence.

Bhakti is derived from Sanskrit "bhaj-" meaning "to worship, to have recourse to," It signifies a deep attachment, devotion, and fondness for the divine—a faith, or love that manifests as spiritual and religious devotion, offering a path to salvation. Bhakti, or devotion, represents a mystical union between the individual and the divine. It emphasizes transforming one's emotions from negativity to positivity, thereby enriching life with beauty and spiritual fulfillment.

But isn't Bhakti/devotion too old fashioned? Something the young ones don't have time for in their so called busy world.

The notion that Bhakti, is an antiquated concept that has lost its relevance in today's fast-paced world is a common perception indeed. Many young individuals, caught up in the whirlwind of modern life, view devotion as a rustic relic of the past, something that no longer resonates with their values or lifestyle.

However, it's essential to recognize that devotion is not a relic of the past; it's an essential aspect of human nature. Devotion is a fundamental expression of our capacity for love, compassion, and connection. It's the fuel that drives us to strive for our highest potential, to serve others, and to leave a lasting impact on the world.

In fact, devotion is more relevant today than ever. With the increasing pace of technological advancements and social media saturation, many individuals are struggling to find meaning and purpose in their lives. They're searching for a deeper sense of connection and fulfillment that transcends the superficial aspects of modern life.

Bhakti offers a profound antidote to this ongoing crisis. By embracing devotion as a spiritual practice, one can cultivate a deeper sense of inner peace, self-awareness, and connection to something greater than oneself. This can lead to a more authentic, meaningful life, characterized by compassion, empathy, and service to others.

So, while it's true that devotion may not be as immediately apparent in modern society as it once was, it's far from being old-fashioned or irrelevant. In fact, it's more necessary now than ever. In an era dominated by speed and efficiency, devotion offers a chance to slow down, connect with our deeper selves, and rediscover the beauty of meaningful relationships. By embracing devotion as a spiritual practice, we can cultivate a sense of inner peace and purpose that transcends the transitory nature of modern life. As we navigate the complexities of contemporary life, we would do well to rekindle our capacity for devotion, recognizing it as a powerful force that can bring us closer to ourselves, each other, and the world around us.

Cultivating Bhakti in Daily Life

Bhakti cannot come by rationalization, it cannot come from knowledge. It comes only with HIS blessings, like it came to me after almost half a century.

It's like Bhakti from Blessing & Blessings from Bhakti.

Nothing happens without HIS blessings.

Before embarking on the path of bhakti, one requires HIS blessings for the very thought to even enter one's mind and once you receive HIS blessings, one can start with a simple daily routine, even if it's just for 5 -10 minutes a day.

- To cultivate a profound devotion to Lord Shiva, start by dedicating a few moments each day to quiet contemplation. Close your eyes and visualize the majestic form of Lord Shiva
- Feel his presence enveloping you, and allow yourself to be filled with his divine light. You may also recite sacred mantras, such as "Om Namah Shivaya," to connect with his energy and you can do this any time, anywhere even in your mind not necessary that you have to sit in a separate place or a temple to recite the mantra.
- Take deep breaths, letting go of all negativity and distractions. Focus your mind on the mantra and allow yourself to be transported to a state of inner peace and transformation.
- To deepen your understanding of Lord Shiva's teachings, read books on his mythology and philosophy, such as the Shiv Purana or writings by renowned gurus. These texts

offer a treasure trove of wisdom and insights into the mysteries of the universe.

- Visit sacred sites associated with Lord Shiva, such as Varanasi or the Jyotirlinga temples or temples on high altitudes. These pilgrimages can be transformative experiences that bring you closer to the divine and nature & of course a good holiday to relax yourself too.
- In addition to personal devotion, strive to serve others through acts of charity and compassion by helping those in need, showing kindness to animals, or offering food and other forms of sustenance to those in need as per your capacity.
- As for having a guru to guide you , Mahesh guruji says "Seek Mahakal as your guru as no human is worthy enough to show the path to bhakti. If HE is the guru he will make situations where you will meet people who will guide you in your pursuit of Bhakti".

Note: These practices are suggestions; everyone approaches devotion in their unique way. There are no strict rules; one can start with a few of these practices or adapt them as they see fit. The essence lies in personal connection and sincere devotion to the divine and in following HIS principles.

Bhakti is also not about renouncing the world or abandoning one's responsibilities to seek enlightenment in solitude. Lord Shiva, the epitome of devotion, is a shining example of how to balance worldly duties with spiritual pursuits. Despite being a family man with a loving wife, Parvati, and children, Ganesh, Kartikeya, and Ashok Sundari, he still finds time for meditation and seclusion.

Similarly, meditation doesn't mean shutting out the world and getting lost in thoughts. It's about carving out moments for oneself (The Me Time as is called today in social media), acknowledging one's own needs and desires. By doing so, we can cultivate inner peace, clarity, and a deeper connection with the divine. In essence, bhakti is about embracing a balanced approach to life, where we tend to our inner selves while still fulfilling our responsibilities and connecting with others.

As I look back on the past five decades of my life, I am reminded of the numerous experiences that have shaped me. In my earlier years, I approached bhakti in a traditional manner, visiting temples, offering flowers and sweets in puja rituals, and bathing in the sacred river Ganges. For me, bhakti was deeply rooted in idol worship, where I would seek solace and connection with the divine through his idols.

Well those, it seems, were all false illusions.

Devotion, or bhakti, is not about rejecting the world or mindlessly idolizing a deity, but rather is a tool to enhance one's life. It's a path to improve our "karma", find inner peace, and cultivate discipline, balance, and foresight. At its core, bhakti is about forming a profound connection with the divine and striving for personal transformation and growth.

You can create your own unique relationship with your chosen deity. Bhakti is simply a means to connect with the divine on your own terms. The beauty of devotion lies in its transformative power. As you cultivate it, you'll develop qualities like humility, love, compassion, and gratitude.

Bhakti encourages one to engage in selfless actions (Karma yoga) with devotion, letting go of attachments to outcomes. This practice helps one transcend the ego and find true fulfillment. Unlike material possessions that can fade or lose value over time, devotion is a flame that burns bright within, guiding us towards inner peace and growth. Through the profound practice of bhakti, one can attain a sense of inner serenity and tranquility, thereby alleviating the burdens of stress, anxiety, and restlessness. This timeless approach to spiritual growth is particularly essential for today's generation, which is increasingly seeking emotional balance.

Bhakti goes beyond mere rituals or rigid schedules of worship. Instead, bhakti is a path that nurtures a loving relationship not only with the divine, but also with oneself and others. It is a journey that cultivates compassion, empathy, and kindness, leading to a deeper sense of connection and harmony with the world around us.

Parvesh Rathi

Noida

"With Mahakal's Darshan, I have felt such positive vibes that all the negativity within me has completely disappeared. From that day until today, it has been three years. The day I had Mahakal's darshan on that very day, I dedicated myself to Lord Shiva and started wearing a Rudraksha bead. It has been three years since I first visited and the vibes I felt from within were incredible. You'll feel a sense of devotion and understand what you might be doing wrong."

Ridheshwar Singh

Hajaribad, Jharkhand

"I feel Mahakal is a different experience, a strong feeling like a vibration when you are in front of Mahakal, it can't be expressed but only felt, but yes something positive happens inside you. I felt something change within me. I felt happy as if I have nothing to worry from now on. Why worry when we have only a few years to live? I realized this in Mahakal Baba's presence. "

CHAPTER 13

Unlocking the Power of Shiv Mantras

Mantra chanting is a sacred gift to mankind. They are an ancient treasure with the capacity to change the present and dissolve all our sufferings when chanted with faith and devotion.

Om Namah S´iva¯ya Mantra

"Om Namah Shivaya" is a powerful mantra dedicated to Lord Shiva in any and every form. It appears in the Yajur Veda.

The mantra "Om Namah Shivaya" is referred to as the Panchakshara Mantra. "Panchakshara" means a mantra consisting of five syllables, and in this case, it consists of the syllables "Om," "Na," "Ma," "Shi," and "Va" (or "Ya") also corresponding to the five elements of nature i.e. agni, jal, vayu, earth & aakash (fire, water, air, earth, space). It is a salutation or reverence to Lord Shiva.

Om: Om is a sacred sound and a spiritual symbol in Hinduism. It represents the essence of the ultimate reality, consciousness, and the universe itself.

Namah: This Sanskrit word means "adoration," "homage," or "bowing down." It signifies offering respect or salutations.

Shivaya: This word means "the auspicious one," referring to Lord Shiva.

So,

ॐ नमःशविाय means "I Bow down to Shiva". In a way, it means bowing down to your own self as Shiva resides in all as own consciousness.

Together, "Om Namah Shivaya" expresses reverence and devotion to Lord Shiva. As we chant Om Namah Shivaya we invite the transformative powers of Shiva to guide us on our spiritual journey dispelling obstacles and illuminating our path towards self-realization, purifying our mind and bringing inner calm.

What happens when you chant Lord Shiva's mantra Om Namah Shivaya?

When you chant the mantra "Om Namah Shivaya", several things occur. Research suggests that combining meditation with chanting improves concentration and memory. The repetitive rhythm of the chant has a positive impact on the brain, which can be beneficial for managing stress, epilepsy, and other neurological conditions. Specifically, chanting "Om Namah Shivaya" has been shown to have a profound effect on the mind, significantly reducing hypertension. Additionally, it increases oxygen levels in the blood, which helps alleviate fatigue.

Beyond physiological benefits, chanting this mantra also helps with emotional and mental issues like anxiety and sadness. It also brings a deep sense of calm and peace, which is good for our overall wellbeing and mental health.

MAHAMRITUNJAY JAAP

The great mantra also known as Tryambakam Mantra/Marita Sanjivani mantra /Rudra Mantra dedicated to Lord Mahakal as Mrityunjaya is found in the Rig Veda where it is attributed to sage Vasishtha.

It is considered one of the most potent and important mantras in Hinduism. Rishis have called it the heart of vedas.

In the Markandeya Purana, a Sanskrit text, the story of Markandeya and the Mahamrityunjaya Mantra is narrated. In ancient times, sage Mrikandu, a devoted follower of Lord Shiva, was blessed with immense knowledge by Shiva. Despite his wisdom, he was saddened by his lack of children. He performed penance to please Shiva and was granted a son named Markandeya, who inherited his father's knowledge and devotion.

As Markandeya grew up, his father revealed the prophecy that he would live a short life. Undeterred, Markandeya dedicated himself to Shiva, composing the powerful Mahamrityunjaya mantra. He chanted it tirelessly for years, clinging to a Shivlinga and refusing to let go.

Yamraj, the god of death, was unable to claim Markandeya's soul due to the mantra's immense power. Shiva was pleased with Markandeya's devotion and granted him a long life. The Mahamrityunjaya mantra became Shiva's favourite due to its creator, Markandeya, who had unlocked its secrets through his unyielding devotion.

The mantra :

ॐ त्र्यम्बकं यजामहे सुगन्धिं पुष्टिवर्धनम ।

उर्वारुकमिव बन्धनान्मृत्योर्मुक्षीय मामृतात् ॥

Om Tryambakam Yajamahe Sugandhim Pushtivardhanam |

Urvarukamiva Bandhanan Mrityor Mukshiya Maamritat | |

Meaning:

Om: The sacred sound representing the essence of the ultimate reality.

Tryambakam: The three-eyed one, referring to Lord Shiva.

Yajamahe: We worship, adore, or invoke.

Sugandhim: The fragrant one, who nourishes all beings like a fragrance.

Pushtivardhanam: The one who enhances prosperity (pushti) and nourishment.

Urvarukamiva: Like the cucumber (urvaruka), which is released (iva) from its bondage (bandhana). This phrase symbolizes liberation from the cycle of birth and death.

Bandhanan: Bondage, specifically referring to the bondage of samsara (the cycle of birth and death).

Mrityor: From death.

Mukshiya: May he liberate.

Ma: Not.

Amritat: Immortality or liberation.

"We meditate on the three-eyed one (Lord Shiva), who is fragrant and who nourishes all beings. May he liberate us from the bondage of worldly attachments, like a ripe cucumber falling off from its vine. May he liberate us from the fear of death, and grant us immortality."

This mantra doesn't give immorality. According to Lord Shiva, those who take birth have to die.

The Maha Mrityunjaya mantra is known for its ability to protect and heal the physical body. It is said that by chanting this sacred mantra, one can strengthen their immune system, boost energy levels, and speed up the healing process of injuries and illnesses. Invoking Shiva's divine presence offers a safeguard against an untimely death by providing protection against illnesses, accidents, calamities, and unexplained situations.

Mahesh Pujari ji, Vijay Pujari ji, Akaash Pujari ji, and other learned individuals also confirmed that they had personally witnessed people reviving and getting better after reciting the Mahamritunjay mantra, although they also acknowledged that death is inevitable. However, they agree that this mantra can help to some extent, not in defeating death, but in overcoming untimely death and prolonging life a little bit. It is believed that this mantra was even used to heal injured soldiers in ancient India.

Gautam Singh Rathod

student, Indore

**"Mei to nadaan hoon, duniya se bhi anjaana hoon...
Par ye sach hei Bhole mei tera deewana hoon."**

"Shiva tells me to control my anger, he teaches me to live a simple life even if I attain all the wealth I desire, He teaches me to be happy from within. Whenever I have the darshan of Mahakal Baba I feel refreshed as if someone has put a new set of batteries in me and I am fully charged with positivity. Whenever I visit Mahakal something good always happens and if ever I pray for something Baba Mahakal always grants my wish. I feel Mahakal is like my father. He always gives me whatever I wish for and always guides me on the right path."

Pooja Belvanshi

MBA student

"This is my 10th time coming for Baba Mahakal's darshan. I am a Shiv bhakt But it was only when I grew up I came to know about Ujjain and Mahakal. Everything is here I feel ever since I have come here positive things keep happening in my life .I feel a vibe here which I have not felt anywhere else. All I can say is if you have faith in Baba Mahakal your life will definitely change for the better."

CHAPTER 14

Revisiting Mahakal's Timeless Wisdom in Contemporary Times

With every darshan of Mahakal I found myself drawn towards Shiva and His teachings. I feel His ancient wisdom continues to resonate with even greater significant relevance in contemporary times, defying cultural and temporal boundaries. His timeless knowledge transcends the ages, offering insights that remain universally applicable and have the power to deeply impact our lives, reshaping our thoughts and outlook towards the world.

In today's fast-paced world, we often obsess over material possessions and external validation, believing they bring happiness. But this chase often leaves us feeling empty and unfulfilled. Even those who seem to have it all, like movie stars, struggle with inner peace. Shiva, the god of detachment, teaches us that true happiness comes from simple things in life, not from material possessions. He reminds us that chasing after these things can leave us feeling empty and unsatisfied.

Shiva's life is the best example which shows that materialism is a veil that shrouds the human soul, binding us to the fleeting whims of the senses. Like a mirage on the desert sand, it appears enticing and real, but ultimately leads to thirst and desolation. Shiva's teachings urge us to pierce this veil, to awaken to the truth that lies beyond the confines of the material world. The attachment to material possessions and desires imprisons us in a cycle of craving and dissatisfaction, preventing us from experiencing the freedom and ecstasy that comes from embracing the infinite.

Shiva's wisdom reminds us that true happiness and fulfillment can only be found by transcending this attachment. As Bholenath, Shiva encourages us to let go of fleeting desires and focus on what truly brings us joy. Shiva invites us to appreciate the beauty of nature, spend time with loved ones, and cultivate inner peace. He is a reminder that innocence is not something to be ashamed of, but rather something to be proud of and that simplicity is strength and not a weakness. By embracing simplicity and innocence, we can find a deep and lasting happiness that comes from within.

Shiva's teachings guide us towards a higher perspective, where we recognize that true wealth lies not in accumulating possessions, but in cultivating inner wisdom, compassion, and awareness. In this world, all things are subject to change and decay. The pursuit of material possessions is like chasing shadows; they appear real for a moment, but vanish like morning mist. Shiva's teachings urge us to focus on the eternal and imperishable, the unshakeable foundation of our being. So, let us leave materialism behind, like a worn-out cloak. Let us don the mantle of truth, and awaken to our true nature. Let us surrender our attachment to the fleeting and focus on the eternal.

Shiva's life was marked by his detachment from material possessions and worldly desires. He renounced his royal throne and lived a simple life in the mountains, showing that true happiness can come only from within and not from material possessions.

In today's age dominated by Instagram and societal expectations, our happiness is often dictated by external benchmarks. We're conditioned to measure success against predefined norms like career choices, marital status, material possessions, and societal timelines. These external pressures can obscure our true sense of happiness and fulfillment, leading us to believe that deviating from these norms is equal to failure. In this pursuit of external validation, we risk losing touch with our inner selves, living according to others' standards rather than listening to our own hearts and minds. The relentless chase for approval from others actually disconnects us from our genuine desires and aspirations.

Shiva, the Adiyogi challenges the conventional notion of success. Renowned for his solitary contemplation in the mountains without material possessions, Shiva can be viewed as a societal failure by modern standards. It doesn't matter whether society considers you a failure or not unless you don't fall in your own eyes.

In today's society, we often find ourselves judging others by rigid beauty standards. The cosmetics industry sells products that claim to transform our physical appearance to fit societal norms. Meanwhile, newspaper matrimonial columns repeatedly advertise for "tall, slim, and fair" brides. In stark contrast, the ancient Hindu deity Shiva stands as a testament to the futility of these external standards. Depicted as a naked ascetic, Shiva defies the societal norms of beauty and status, embodying the concept of "Mahadev" - the highest of the gods. Despite his unconventional physical appearance, with his blue-skinned body, Shiva is revered as Neelkanth. This serves as a powerful reminder to live authentically, free from the need for external validation. In today's world, where social media platforms often lead to feelings of inadequacy and body shaming, particularly among young women, Shiva's philosophy is more relevant than ever. Instead of conforming to societal beauty standards, young girls should draw inspiration from Shiva's unapologetic approach to life. By embracing their true selves, they can cultivate a sense of self-worth that is unshakeable. Shiva's timeless message serves as a beacon of hope, encouraging us to break free from the shackles of societal expectations and live life on our own terms.

In the revered texts of Hindu mythology, the deity Shiva is often depicted as someone who upholds truth and righteousness. Despite his benevolent nature, Shiva is not afraid to take a stand against injustice and wrongdoing examples being, Ravana, Andhaka the demon or Lord Brahma. Ravana, a devotee of Shiva who had received divine blessings, committed the egregious act of abducting Sita, leading to his downfall at the hands of Lord Ram. This serves as a stark reminder that even the most favored among the gods are not immune to the consequences of their actions, illustrating that while Shiva may bestow blessings upon his devotees, he does not condone unjust actions. Instead, Shiva steadfastly upholds truth and righteousness. Shiva's unwavering commitment to truth and righteousness is further confirmed by His punishment to Brahma for his wrongdoings when He cut off Brahma's 5th head for the wrongs committed showing that he was willing to make difficult choices to stay true to himself and his values. And in this fake world we need to stay true to ourselves and learn to make difficult choices in unfavorable situations.

Shiva's consumption of HALAHALA, a potent poison symbolizing darkness, during the churning of the ocean, is another testament to his unwavering resolve. By consuming this poison, Shiva safeguarded the Earth and demonstrated that even in the face of adversity, there is always hope for a brighter future. It's a powerful reminder that darkness is merely the absence of light and that challenges and struggles can be transformative. Shiva, known as Rudra in the Vedas, signifies the deity of anger, highlighting that Mahadev can experience anger akin to humans. His cosmic dance, the Tandav, holds the power to potentially destroy the world.

Then should we show our anger and destroy everything?

No, anger itself is not inherently negative; its impact depends on how we harness it. Much like a sword, improperly wielded anger can harm us. However, when directed constructively, anger becomes a potent force for transformation. Today's generation frequently experiences quick and intense anger towards various triggers.

Shiva teaches us the importance of pausing instead of reacting impulsively. Stepping back to assess the situation enables us to respond thoughtfully, leading to more favorable outcomes having the potential to positively transform our lives by teaching us that we need to channelize our energy in the right direction and at the right time.

Shiva's steady dedication and focus are also exemplary. His meditation and self-discipline indicate the importance of devotion and concentration in achieving our goals by staying committed even in the face of distractions, no matter how tempting the distractions may be, thus teaching us that determination and focus are the keys to overcoming obstacles and reaching our goals. Shiva, as Adiyogi, the primal yogi, imparted the profound knowledge of yoga to his consort Parvati in a systematic manner establishing himself as Adiyogi—the pioneer of yoga which not only aids in physical fitness but also fosters mental strength and well-being, improves concentration and helps focus on our goals.

But today's youth is often misguided, prioritizing fleeting pleasures over meaningful goals. In their quest for temporary highs they are increasingly resorting to the consumption of substances like bhang misusing them for recreational purposes rather than understanding their cultural significance and medicinal benefits. It is essential to recognize that Lord Shiva's consumption of Bhang and Dhatura was a manifestation of his divine nature and to be revered as offering to Him not for recreational use. Mahakal encourages us to accept life's natural cycles, including death and impermanence, helping us cherish the present and cope with uncertainty rather than going in for short term pleasures. In fact HE teaches us to be creative. His Damru & his Tandav dance are the first creative art forms of this Earth. So why indulge in wrong deeds when there is so much good to create with our immense talent.

Shiva is often depicted with various symbols which are not just for mere decoration but convey a deeper meaning of spirituality and self-realization. Actually it is not just Shiva's philosophies but every tiny detail related to Shiva imparts important lessons of life. His trishul (trident) reminds one to balance thoughts, emotions, and actions to achieve inner peace and outer success. Shiva's third eye represents wisdom, intuition, and the power of inner vision teaching us about perception beyond the physical realm and the ability to see beyond illusion and to be aware of our thoughts, emotions, and actions. It's like having a sense of intuition that guides us to make wise decisions. The Vasuki snake coiled thrice around Shiva's neck symbolizes not just the trinity of past, present, and future time but also alertness. The Rudraksha beads are a symbol of Shiva's blessings and are worn by devotees as a means of protection and used for meditation and spiritual growth along with having medicinal value. The sacred river Ganga which flows from Shiva's hair locks reminds us about the flow of divine grace and the cleansing of impurities within us. Nandi is a living lesson on patience, devotion, strength, righteousness, spiritual aspiration, and the sacred relationship between humans and animals in Hindu tradition. The pure white snow-clad Kailash Mountain where Shiva resided is a symbol of purity of mind. The sacred ash symbolizes renunciation of ego and worldly attachments and teaches us that everything in the material world is temporary and that death is the ultimate reality of life.

Mahakal teaches us to let go, to release and find inner peace. HE reminds us to be brave and true to ourselves, teaching us to live in the moment and cherish every breath. He shows us that we need to face our fears and let go of things that hold us back.

Mahakal helps us see that everything is connected and that there's more to life than what we can see. He's the guide for those who want to change and grow, to look beyond what's fake and find wisdom and peace. He inspires us to discover ourselves and make positive changes in our lives.

Mahakal is a journey to know ourselves better.

Not an end but a beginning.......

What I discovered during Mahakal's darshan was profound. It was not just a pilgrimage to a sacred place, but an odyssey into oneself, forging a connection with Mahakal.

Mahakal transcends mere bliss and connecting with Mahakal goes beyond simple devotion. As I reflect on Mahakal's essence I feel it has led me towards complete dissolution, shattering my veil of ignorance into pieces.

As I come to the end of this journey or rather I would call it a beginning of a new journey of starting to get to know Shiva and a bit of myself too, I am left with a profound sense of awe and reverence. The Lord of Time and Death, Mahakal, has revealed to me the happiness I had been seeking for so long and all who have been blessed with Mahakal's darshan have been transformed by the experience. He has taught me that change is the only constant in an ever-changing world and that life is but a fleeting moment, that our time on earth is short so we need to live in the present and make the best use of it instead of getting caught in our ego and desires.

I am left with a sense of gratitude for the wisdom I have gained in my journey so far being inspired to live my life with renewed purpose.

Mahakal is not just a mythological figure, but a reflection of our own capacity for transformation. HE is a reminder that we have the potential to transcend our own limitations and become the best version of ourselves. HE symbolizes the power within us to break free from the chains of our own making and rise above the constraints that hold us back, allowing us to realize our true potential. We all have within us the power to rise from the ashes like a phoenix and dance once more in harmony with the cosmos.

As I close this book on Mahakal, I am left with a sense of hope and optimism. I know that no matter what challenges I may face, no matter what darkness I may encounter, Mahakal will guide the way.

And so, let us take one final bow to Mahakal, and thank him for showing us the way.